The Invent To Learn Guide to Fun

The Invent To Learn Guide To Fun

Josh Burker

Constructing Modern Knowledge Press

For information on direct or volume sales, contact the publisher:

Constructing Modern Knowledge Press

21825 Barbara St.

Torrance, CA 90503

www.CMKPress.com | sales@cmkpress.com

CRA043000   CRAFTS & HOBBIES / Crafts for Children

EDU029030   EDUCATION / Teaching Methods & Materials / Science & Technology

ISBN: 978-0-9891511-8-4

Series editor: Sylvia Libow Martinez

Layout and cover design: Yvonne Martinez

Important note to readers:

Like anything that's fun, the projects in this book involve a risk of things going wrong. Please take into account your own skill level, comfort with electronics or tools, and many other conditions. Different people will find different projects easy or difficult depending on many factors and experience. Do not undertake a project that makes you feel uncomfortable. The author and publisher cannot and do not accept any responsibility for any damages, injuries, or losses as a result of following the steps and information in this book. Always obey law, codes, policies, manufacturer's instructions, and observe safety precautions. Use common sense and have fun!

Contents

Projects

Project	Software	Hardware	Supplies
Squishy Circuit Experiments			Homemade dough, LEDs, batteries
LEGO ArtBots	Scratch	computer, LEGO WeDo Kit	
Animated Postcards			Paper, LEDs, batteries, copper tape
MaKey MaKey Musical Instruments	Scratch	computer, MaKey MaKey	
MaKey MaKey Operation Game	Scratch	computer, MaKey MaKey	
Soft Circuit Stuffed Animals			Sewing supplies, conductive thread, LEDs, battery
TurtleArt Experiments	TurtleArt	computer	
Glowdoodlers	Glowdoodle, TinkerCAD*	computer, 3D Printer*	
Chain Reaction Machines	Scratch	LEGO WeDo, computer	Recycled toys, building supplies
Carnival Games	Scratch		
Turtle Art Tiles	TurtleArt, TinkerCAD	computer, 3D Printer	Firing or air-hardening clay*
Dungeon Crawl Adventure Game	Scratch	computer, Picoboard	
Crystal Radio Receiver		3D Printer*	Electrical supplies

* Optional

Note: All projects also use a variety of easy-to-find electronics, recyclables, office supplies, and craft materials. See each project for a specific supply list.

The Case for Fun

As an educator, I have thought at length about the role play and fun serves in the modern classroom. By "classroom" I mean any space where learning happens. The classroom might be in a school with a small or large group of students, a maker space, a library, a community center, a kitchen table, or in a workshop you facilitate. The projects in this book have been thoroughly workshopped in all of these spaces, with people ranging in age from six to eighty-eight.

Play is real learning

In Kindergarten, students come into school in the best position to learn because they typically have had time for playful exploration, invention, and unstructured play. A traditional Kindergarten encourages students to learn by creating knowledge through playful hands-on learning. Typically, there are many different child-friendly materials with which the students can work. Open-ended toys, like wood blocks, serve a prominent role. Often, there is enough space in the classroom for the children's creations to remain in place, to be worked on over time.

However, as students get older, classrooms get less playful as we insist that children "get serious" about learning. By the time students are in high school they no longer "play" in most of their classrooms. The work, though mature and academic, lacks the personal meaning and the lasting impression of the knowledge created through play in youth. Rather, work in a high school classroom often devolves into learning facts perhaps totally disconnected from the student's personal experience or interests. Often, the material is delivered in a lecture format, with the student seen as a vessel into which the knowledge is transferred. Demonstration of mastery of a topic is reduced to a test or a paper.

While I am not advocating that we abandon all curriculum and aimlessly play in our classrooms, I do think that there is merit to thoughtfully considering the role play serves in your classroom. How scripted is the time you spend talking to your class? How much of the class time is you, and how much is them? Is there any room for serendipitous discoveries to be made, or are you providing the "ah-ha" moments like a magician hitting her or his cues?

Consider: what about play is so engaging? When you play, do you find yourself in the "zone," where time elongates, you find focus and drive, clarity of vision, are able to find an elasticity in the materials which you work, and you have an increased reception to new ideas or perspectives? What about play makes the lessons learned during play so personal and memorable? Can we leverage playfulness and make our boring curriculum more "playful"?

I have led children and adults through successful, playful activities. I have also led people by lecturing, being too theoretical, and explaining everything myself. The more I teach, the more I am convinced that playful activities work better at keeping people's attention, encouraging them to take risks, teaching them new skills, and collaborating.

First, there is a capacity for intensity during play. Recall how difficult it is to end recess, to shift children away from the toys and to wash hands for dinner, or to turn off the video game you are playing. People who are at play find focus in the play. They are entertaining themselves through the activity. Play is imagination-driven. Play encourages you to make things up, to try out new ideas, identities, and inventions. Additionally, in play rules are not externally enforced. That is not to say there are no rules when children are playing, but adults seldom impose the rules on the children who are at play. Instead, the players make up the rules governing the play.

Second, there is flexibility to materials in play. Children in particular, but often adults, too, (by self-limitation), have a limited palette of materials with which they are typically allowed or able to work. A child denied the use of the power hacksaw may be upset, but will go on to invent her own "play" hacksaw to mimic the adult version. The child overcomes the limitations of her palette of workable materials by using her imagination. Cardboard becomes a versatile material for the maker, young and old, because of the facility with which it is cut and worked into different shapes. The ability for the maker to build using materials such as cardboard lowers the barrier to entry. Cardboard's familiarity and approachability also sparks a playful approach to using the material. The cardboard can be easily cut with a blade or even scissors in a crunch.

It also can be painted or colored with a pen or a crayon. The material easily conforms to the maker's imagination. Additionally, cardboard boxes can be found in virtually every dumpster, so the act of playful invention become a sustainable, transformative act.

Third, play creates collaborative possibilities. During play, an "expert" is often identified by the players. This player might be particularly good at building bridges with wooden blocks, at leveling the build plate on the 3D printer, or drawing a good circle. Opportunities for individuals to emerge as leaders because of the skills they have to contribute to play is rewarding and educational. While the group plays and observes the one expert contributing her or his skills to a particularly tricky part of the play, some of the players, too, are learning this coveted skill. Play, and the emergence of specialized skills, has the potential of teaching others to become experts in arcane or important matters related to the play. Finally, playing in a group allows you to accomplish more. The hurdle to build really large objects is lowered with an extra set of hands to help you hold the material. Play can create an inclusive, educational environment which produces more experts through the players' "work."

Play is good for children and adults alike. It promotes intensity, flexible thinking and acting, and collaboration. We should aspire to bring more play into our learning spaces, whether they are in schools, libraries, maker spaces, or our own homes. I hope *The Invent to Learn Guide to Fun* will serve as a valuable resource for you as you increase the fun in your classroom.

Why a Guide to Fun in the Classroom?

I believe that learning happens when people of all ages have fun and are working on projects that engage and challenge them. Learning to facilitate such projects has been my quest and work for the past eight years. I'm excited to share this journey with you.

My Pepperdine Online Master's in Educational Technology (OMET) experience was my first acquaintance with constructivist learning, in which learners construct their knowledge by direct experience. (I share more about this in the next chapter). It immediately inspired me to transform the school technology club to be a more inclusive environment, where girls and students on the autism spectrum could also thrive, opened my eyes to the power of technology to unite people, to provide a (literal) voice, and to make available to students tools they could use to be creative beyond their years. Providing students with physical space, tools, and the opportunity to lead others in projects they devised on their own fostered amazing creativity. Participation by girls increased because projects were designed with collaboration at the forefront. Autistic students were given increased opportunities to collaborate with peers and to assume leadership roles in projects. During OMET I learned the value of providing a context, a space to meet, and technology to use while getting out of the way and allowing students to lead and create.

An additional transformative experience for me has been attending the Constructing Modern Knowledge (CMK) Summer Institute (http://constructingmodernknowledge.com). Here, teachers are encouraged to take off their teacher hats and to put on learning hats. Over four days of "hard fun" participants work in groups or in some cases individually to build fantastic

inventions, contraptions, compositions, and more. Over the course of three different CMK institutes, I build an artbot programmed in MicroWorlds; a LEGO WeDo/Scratch turntable to play real records; a LEGO ukulele strumming jig; a stereoscope viewer that used a smartphone to display the stereoscopic images created with another LEGO jig (a little more than a year before Google's "Cardboard" project!); and a remix of a LEGO WeDo/Scratch robotic arm to create randomized art.

CMK encouraged me to revise much of my curriculum after asking myself, "What would happen if I spent an extended time focused on teaching third grade TurtleArt?" CMK helped me realize the importance of passion and play in learning. Given the opportunity to connect with other people with similar interests, to focus intensely on a project, to rapidly prototype your ideas, to receive feedback and improve your designs, and to share your work with an appreciative audience is an incredibly rewarding and educational experience. By providing students the time to thoroughly tinker with and learn to understand a technology, be it software or hardware, students will find something with which they are intensely focused on understanding. The projects students create while passionately pursuing knowledge of a subject are outstanding.

In June, 2014, I was selected as the Westport Library's Maker-In-Residence. I spent twenty hours at the library over the course of the month helping children and adults construct cardboard, wire, aluminum foil, and copper tape musical instruments, which we connected to computers with MaKey MaKeys and programmed in Scratch. This project combined the ideas I learned in my technology club and at Constructing Modern Knowledge: a space conducive to collaboration and a project dictated by the learner's interests produce remarkable results. An additional element made this project successful: building Scratch MaKey MaKey musical instruments was a perfect intersection of technology and crafting. The people who were initially uncomfortable with the perceived difficulty of the project when they saw the MaKey MaKey and its circuitry came to embrace the opportunity to make the instrument they crafted from upcycled materials make a sound. Working with familiar materials like cardboard or aluminum foil lowered the difficulty of the project and allowed nearly everybody to craft an instrument on their own (of course, young children had help with the box cutter). During my residency I had over 200 individual encounters with individuals, many of whom stayed for the two hours it took to build an instrument, connect it to a computer and program it to play different notes.

I continue to strive to create spaces in which people can collaborate and work on projects that merge crafting and technology. Recently the independent school at which I work established a Maker Studio where my office is now located. I hope for it to be a space where teachers from all divisions can work in groups to learn about the engaging tools and technologies we have at our disposal, and then take them to their own classrooms and create projects that encourage intensity and passionate learning.

This book is written from my experiences in classrooms, workshops, and in my own learning. It serves as a guide to help you create projects for creative, fun learning by people of all ages.

I joked that my Maker-In-Residency workshop was for people ages 8 to 88. It turns out that the gentleman who built the trumpet and performed at the concluding presentation was 88, so he just made the cutoff. The same holds true for this book: it scales from youth to adults. Younger students might benefit from working with an older child or an adult. A good strategy if you find a project too difficult is to work on the project with a partner. Sometimes an extra set of hands or someone else's prior experience can help overcome obstacles.

Each project in this book has a "challenge level." The challenge level indicates the number of materials used, the type of tools used, the length of time it takes to complete a project. Some projects are more challenging than others, but patience, making sure you understand the instructions, and perhaps a partner can help the least experienced person accomplish every project in this book.

If you use this book in a workshop or a classroom, try to let the students do as much work independent of your "helping hands." Each of these projects uses tools that an elementary student, with some training, could use. There might be parts of some projects that leave the students frustrated because they want to reach the conclusion more quickly. Other times they might be frustrated because they lack the skills or ability to accomplish a step in a project. I use Dr. Gary Stager and Sylvia Martinez's distinction, in their book *Invent to Learn: Making, Tinkering, and Engineering in the Classroom*, of "mouth up vs. mouth down frustration." Mouth down frustration amounts to insurmountable challenges to accomplishing a project, for example, broken hardware or software that does not work. Mouth up frustration comes from being pushed to work just beyond your current ability in order to accomplish your goals. Using this book as a guide, you are less likely to encounter mouth down frustration and to provoke many wonderful, educational mouth up frustrating moments.

Working on hands-on projects like these in a classroom or workshop can be challenging because oftentimes the participants have widely varying skills. How do you lead groups through these projects without being pulled in every direction trying to put out fires and answer every request for help? First, whether you are working with young students or adults, dispel the idea that you are the sole possessor of knowledge in the room. The classrooms where I teach often have pods of four students working together. Conveniently, when I ask the students to "ask three before me," they have three potential experts sitting at the table with them. If you let the students talk among themselves, get up out of their seats to assist others, and you leverage the willingness of some students to help others, you instantly have more sets of hands and minds to help.

Building in time at the beginning of a project for unguided free exploration encourages students to discover the technology at their own speed and to share their serendipitous discoveries about how the technology works. Children in particular love making discoveries and sharing them. Leveraging this enthusiasm at the beginning of a project uncovers the parts of the hardware or software the students find most interesting. The projects in this book are engaging and customizable and once the students get going you will find them intensely tinkering, building, and sharing. There are always students who rush to a conclusion and expect a reward. I try to set the expectation that in my classes the project is never finished. A person can always take what they have made and make it bigger, longer in duration, or make a different one using a different construction technique or materials.

How to use this book

The projects in this book vary in the amount of involvement and the time it takes to complete a project. You can find a project to work on in the timeframe you have available. There are short projects that you can complete in an afternoon. Other projects are broken into manageable segments that can be worked on over the course of a school term or during a school vacation.

The materials used in the projects have a low barrier to entry, but with each project there is room to grow and take your creation to the next level. For example, your first iteration might be made of cardboard, but your final iteration may include 3D printed components.

The projects in *The Invent To Learn Guide to Fun* encourage play and collaboration. Some projects encourage others to contribute a part, like one of the programming projects in the book. Other projects involve you making something tangible that others can play with or use to make something of their own. You will find that nobody is sitting around when they are working on a project in this book—there are many roles to play, parts to build, and much fun to be had.

Like anything that's fun, the projects in this book involve a risk of things going wrong. Please take into account your own skill level, comfort with electronics or tools, and many other conditions. Different people will find different projects easy or difficult depending on unique factors and experience. Do not undertake a project that makes you feel uncomfortable, but don't always stay in your comfort zone. Always obey law, codes, policies, manufacturer's instructions, and observe safety precautions. Use common sense and have fun!

Each of the projects in *The Invent To Learn Guide to Fun* is remixable, so make changes that personalize your project and make it your own. Share your remixes on social media and teach us a new way to play with the projects. Most of all, with the *Invent To Learn Guide to Fun* in hand, go out there and have a good time!

Technology is always changing...

We have made every attempt at accuracy while writing this book. Technology will advance, products will be updated or even disappear, software will have new versions, and URLs are likely to break.

To save space and knowing that you cannot click on a book, we have shortened some very long URLs using Bitly.com which will redirect you to the actual URL. We hope this website remains active! Resources and URLs in this book can be found here: cmkpress.com/fun.

Hard Fun

I first became acquainted with Seymour Papert's concept of "hard fun" as a student of Dr. Gary Stager's in 2006. The ten "Learning Adventures" he challenged my Pepperdine University Online Master's in Educational Technology (OMET) cadre to take were vexing, outside of many of our fields of experience or expertise, and challenged us to collaborate despite physical distance from one another. Many of us had never played a musical instrument, but we were challenged to use Finale musical notation software to compose a musical piece. One Learning Adventure, where we were asked to examine the Collatz Conjecture (also called the 3n problem), was so difficult yet so engaging that I cornered a math teacher at a birthday party and talked with him for an hour about the problem and how best to analyze the data Dr. Stager taught us to generate.

> To see how I used the MicroWorlds EX software to generate numbers and Microsoft Excel to graph the 3n data, visit http://cmkpress.com/fun/3n.

I recall the vexation that some of my classmates and I felt with these learning challenges. The Learning Adventures had no definitive answers. Our anxiety to achieve in this graduate education course caused us to believe that Dr. Stager was somehow looking for a "correct" answer to the assignments. We were challenged to compose music, create podcasts (this was 2006, and most people had yet to start subscribing to podcasts, let alone creating them), and argue whether Ned Kelly (an Australian Robin Hood type) was a hero or a villain.

As hard as some of us searched, there was no "right" answer to any of these Learning Adventures. Rather, the exploration of a beautiful piece of astronomy software, like Celestia, or watching *Comedian*, the film about Jerry Seinfeld that Dr. Stager called the best example of

> The OMET program is now named Master's in Learning Technology (MALT) and remains an intense, transformative one-year online Master's Degree in Education program offered by Pepperdine University.

a community of practice and of situated learning theories ever captured on film, provided opportunities to explore topics new to many of us. Exploring an idea without a notion of how one "solves" the problem is a powerful educational opportunity. Learners who are encouraged to explore and document how one approaches, turns over, and plays with the problem emerge from a Learning Adventure with a more flexible attitude to answering a challenge, solving a problem, or persuading others to a viewpoint.

Once I learned to embrace the adventure and find joy in being stymied because I was under no pressure to devise a "correct" solution, I began to understand what Gary meant when he kept mentioning "hard fun" as we complained about the difficulty of some of the Learning Adventures.

Figuring out that Dr. Stager wasn't after any one single answer to the Learning Adventures made the class a little more fun, but there was no getting around the fact the Learning Adventures were still hard. After all, each Learning Adventure seemed to bring us further outside our immediate areas of knowledge. We were teachers, business people, students, managers, and we were being challenged to create projects about history, the solar system, and computer programming.

At least with one project, where we were asked to use MicroWorlds EX to program turtles to draw quilt patterns, I had some immediate familiarity: I had briefly programmed Logo in elementary school, and my mother is a quilter. Still this Learning Adventure required me and my cadre to learn (or re-learn) Logo programming. Dr. Stager has been instrumental in keeping Logo in the conversation about teaching children to program since the 1980s. In this whimsical challenge, we had to program not only our quilt square, but load our classmates' turtles into our MicroWorld and choreograph them to build an entire quilt from the turtles' procedures. Some of us had to dust off long-forgotten Logo programming skills, while others learned Logo for the first time. A true "low floor, high ceiling" computer programming language, most everyone was able to create unique, colorful, and collaborative turtle procedures. To make this project a little less hard and a little more fun, we needed to learn new tools. The success of a "hard fun" project depends on access to a large toolbox of tools, whether they are digital in this case, or physical, in the case of a 3D printing project. Success also depends on using the right tool for the right reasons for the right project.

> Here is the explanation of how I designed my quilt square and programmed my classmates' turtles to create a quilt: http://cmkpress.com/fun/quilt

As the Pepperdine course peaked and we were really rolling on the Learning Adventures, we found the secret to achieving the maximum "hard fun" from the Learning Adventures. Since the Pepperdine program was nearly entirely online, we used different tools, both synchronous and asynchronous, to keep in touch with one another and conduct our classes.

The more we collaborated, the richer the Learning Adventure became. Even though we were physically separated, we were programming turtles that performed in harmony, generating and sharing huge samples of data to explore Collatz's "3n Problem" looking for repeating patterns, and arguing over the martyr-hood of the Chicago 7.

> Immediately after attending the opening Virt Camp at Pepperdine's campus I flew to London to join my wife, who was finishing her degree. I met for classes on my laptop in the middle of the night from Oxford, a farmhouse in Aix-en-Provence, and a hotel lobby in Barcelona, anywhere with wifi!

Participation and the exchange of hard ideas created the atmosphere of "hard fun" Gary kept promising us when we pushed back at the difficulty of the challenges. The authentic need to collaborate in these Learning Adventures created engagement and deeper understanding of the topic of the Adventure. Without collaboration, we would not have a pool of data or an audience to listen to a podcast about changing my diet and teaching you a new recipe.

If I distilled my understanding of "hard fun" into an easy to explain idea, it is an engaging open-ended project that pushes your skills to create knowledge that is shared.

Trust me, Meg's Eggplant Lasagne recipe is well worth listening to the podcast: http://cmkpress.com/fun/recipe

This book is a collection of "hard fun" projects intended to help you find fun as you build skills, make things with your hands and the technology around you, and create learning environments where people collaborate around a project to further the design, use, and function of the tools you create. While some of the projects in this book can be built and used solitarily, they are most fun when brought into classrooms, conference anterooms, or your home, where many people can collaborate and express their creativity. Sharing the process and the tools reveals new uses and spawns remixes.

Adults like to have fun too! The Glowdoodlers I built and brought to the PopTech conference were a big hit one morning among the attendees, in a dim waiting room in the Camden, Maine Opera House. We traced the edges of the room and furniture with different colors and captured the images in Glowdoodle on my laptop.

Where Do Good Project Ideas Come From?

When I talk to people about what I do with the students I teach or in the workshops I facilitate, people often ask me where I got the idea to program to create ceramic tiles or use LED
Glowdoodlers to draw a night sky so Kindergarten students could find and create their own
constellations. My inspiration comes from finding a tool that is whimsical and works well
enough to trust it will not break when I put it in a room full of kids, which takes the fun out
of the project and amplifies the hard. Test the software you plan to use in your classroom or
workshop ahead of time: make sure it saves or exports without crashing. The benefit of building
your own tools, like a Glowdoodler, is that when it breaks through use you know how to repair
it. I also look for tools that help lower the barrier to making something phenomenal. The MaKey
MaKey musical instruments is such a tool. Few of us are great musicians, fewer still know
how to build an instrument. However, tools like the MaKey MaKey lower the barrier to being a
musician and building a musical instrument.

Likewise, I try to look for (or build) tools that allow the inner workings to be seen, so that
people can adapt them with individual expression. TurtleArt is a wonderful software tool, a
learning environment that allows for total self-expression using a common vocabulary and
set of commands. One student's creation can be easily loaded into another student's TurtleArt
program for exploration and remixing. Likewise, the Scratch programming software is built
on being able to see how the code works and sharing clever sets of code blocks with a huge
community to expand the software's capabilities and usefulness.

Many of my projects use "upcycled" materials, such as cardboard and packaging that can be
cleverly repurposed. Rather than buying specialized kits or believing a 3D printer is necessary,
try working with the materials you readily have at hand. Certainly, some projects requires
specialized parts, like LEDs or the LEGO WeDo kit. When considering purchasing a part, kit, or
tool, ask yourself if it serves a single purpose or can it be used in other activities. One reason

why I do not immediately break out the finger LED toys when my classes start playing with Glowdoodle is because I would rather give them coin cell batteries, LEDs, wire, copper tape, and cardboard and see what they can make from the materials without any preconceived designs in mind. Each of these projects encourages you to be a creator, not a consumer.

...And Then?

In a typically provocative blog post (http://stager.tv/blog/?p=3214) Gary Stager challenged educators to ask themselves, "...and then?" in order to "...[encourage/require] teachers to extend the activity that much further." I read this post right before I started my Maker-In-Residency, in which I helped around 200 people build MaKey MaKey musical instruments and program them in Scratch over the course of a month. It completely changed the scope of my project and resulted in some amazing creations.

> This video features many of the MaKey MaKey instruments. http://vimeo.com/100175635

Try creating projects where the students go on to create something with the new tool they built. The 3D Printed TurtleArt tiles project uses many skills: programming, 3D design and Computer Aided Design (CAD), and 3D printing. This project could have easily stopped with the 3D printed TurtleArt procedure, which is beautifully rendered by the printer. The "...and then?" moment was collaborating with the art teacher to create a lesson where the students brought their 3D printed stamps to art class, practiced stamping in Play-Doh then clay, and created ceramic tiles. Once fired, the students took the project even further by selecting glazes and deepening their designs by adding colors. The students would not have been able to create tiles of such complexity without the tool they programmed and 3D printed. Likewise, programming music in Scratch is a lofty project made easier and more concrete by encouraging students to build musical instruments, use a MaKey MaKey to connect them to a computer, and program the instrument to respond to the musician's touch. This project can be further extended by asking people to create songs, develop a method of writing down their songs, and sharing and performing the songs with others. Every project can be extended.

Likewise, "...and then?" can help encourage iteration. I find that with everything I make there is satisfaction with completing the project and seeing how others react to what I have made and how they use it. However, the initial excitement is soon tempered by ideas of how I might improve on the design. Rarely do I throw out a design in its entirety. Rather, I look for more efficient, more reliable, or more easily reproducible ways of completing the project. When evaluating a project of my own, I ask myself, "...and then?" to help me improve the project or object.

A recent project to design a macrophotography focusing jig for the One Laptop Per Child XO-4 Laptop took four iterations over the course of a month to arrive at a design that is easy to print with minimal material and easily constructed once printed.

Always Updating

Make it a goal to take a look at projects you have worked on with fresh eyes and some distance. See if you can find ways to update your projects the next time you teach a class or workshop. Start by observing how people follow the project directions and modify them for ease, because of the materials on hand (or not available), or because they have a better way of constructing something. Observe as you lead workshops for people of different ages. Middle school students have better manual dexterity then elementary students, so any paper circuit building workshops I run use wider copper tape and bigger notecards with the younger students.

Once a project is built and complete, observe how it is used. The Scratch Operation game has a good built-in cheat if the chopsticks are not completely covered in conductive material, like foil or copper tape. Unscrupulous players could take advantage that such a rigged set can safely touch the base of the foil cups. Sometimes a bug is fun to leave in a game, but other times it diminishes the effectiveness or realism of the project. One observation that came from watching students use their 3D printed TurtleArt stamps with Play-Doh is they were intent on creating a tile that used every classmate's stamp. Of course the resulting tile was a mess. But the experiment provided an "...and then?" opportunity: work in groups to design a complex design made through the application of multiple 3D TurtleArt stamps to a single clay tile. By observing the usage of the project you can begin to iterate on the design to build a better version of the tool.

Once your project is in "the wild," shared in your classroom or library, on your blog, and through social media, observe how people remix the project. I was delighted to see graphics I developed for a squishy circuit workshop be mashed up with an Operation Game version, built with paper plates that stored the components and created the game board, and used by teens in Washington D.C. for a summer technology workshop. Remixing provides many opportunities to iterate on a design, and to see how people develop clever alternatives to the way you originally built your project. Scratch is built on the idea of every project being remixable. The MaKey MaKey is "...and then?" hardware because all it does it provide whimsical access to some of the keyboard and leaves it to the user to remix from there.

By documenting your project and sharing it with others you invite people to change, expand, modify, and grow your work. Good documentation includes photographs that illustrate the process so others can reproduce your work. Blogging is a great way to share your successes and failures with projects and provide others with a template, instructions, or blueprints for how to create their own versions of your projects.

Software

This chapter will introduce the software used in some of the projects. All the software is free and works on either the Mac or PC platform. There are many good tutorials available with the software, and additional information is available online.

TurtleArt

TurtleArt (http://turtleart.org) is an easy to use, block-based programming language that allows students to use mathematical reasoning, problem solving, counting, measurement, geometry and computer programming to create beautiful images. It is available by emailing the contact available on their web site. TurtleArt is part of the Logo programming family. At first, it

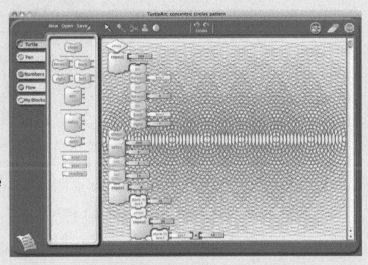

may seem limited in its capabilities compared to other Logo implementations. However, it is easy to use and very powerful because of its elegant simplicity.

TurtleArt comes with a great two-part Getting Started tutorial and some samples and "snippets." Additionally, every image included in the TurtleArt galleries on the web site and the locally installed examples can be dragged and dropped into TurtleArt so you can examine the blocks and procedures. You can easily remix the sample projects, and people can easily remix your projects. If you post full size versions of your TurtleArt files, which save in PNG format, to image sharing websites such as Flickr, people can download the full sized version with the metadata containing the TurtleArt blocks intact for examining and remixing. TurtleArt also comes with a series of cards you can use to learn what the different blocks do and how to combine them to beautiful effect.

Scratch

Scratch is a free programming language available from the MIT Media Lab's Lifelong Kindergarten group. Like Turtle Art, Scratch is a descendant of the Logo programming language that was invented by Dr. Seymour Papert, Cynthia Solomon, and others. These programming languages contain powerful ideas about how children learn that make them particularly relevant for today's classroom.

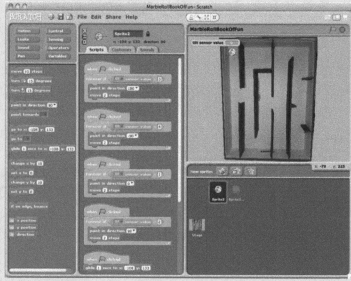

Scratch is available in two versions: Scratch 1.4 (http://scratch.mit.edu/scratch_1.4/) which must be downloaded onto your computer, and Scratch 2.0 (http://scratch.mit.edu) which runs in most browsers and does not require downloading.

I still mostly use Scratch 1.4 in my projects. It is stable and generally will not break when you give it to a room full of users. It does not require an Internet connection. It comes with over one hundred musical instrument sounds. The projects you create in Scratch 1.4 can still be shared to the Scratch website, which converts them to version 2.

Additionally, PicoBoard support is solid in Scratch 1.4, whereas in Scratch 2.0 it was still in development at publication.

Scratch 2.0 does benefit from being cloud-based, so people who use Scratch 2.0 in a workshop go home with their projects online, ready to continue working on them. Of course, it requires an Internet connection and the extra step of creating an account, but these are surmountable challenges.

Inkscape

Inkscape (http://inkscape.org/en/) is the poor man's version of Illustrator. A free vector graphics editor for Windows, Mac OS X, and Linux, this software is used to convert the .png file from TurtleArt to an .svg file for use with TinkerCad. While the software is powerful and complex, the project instructions lead you through a very small subset of tools to produce the file you need.

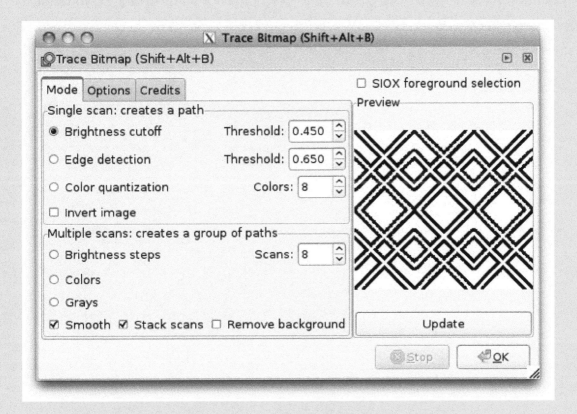

Tinkercad

Tinkercad (http://www.tinkercad.com) is an online 3D modeling Computer Aided Design (CAD) program that is usable by Kindergarten students and adults alike.

You can create 3D models using their pre-made geometric shapes, negative space, and javascript Shape Generators. Additionally, you can import .svg files to extrude and model for 3D printing. Tinkercad is web-based and suffers downtime from time to time, so you should always prepare for the eventuality that the tool might not be available when you go to use it in a class or workshop.

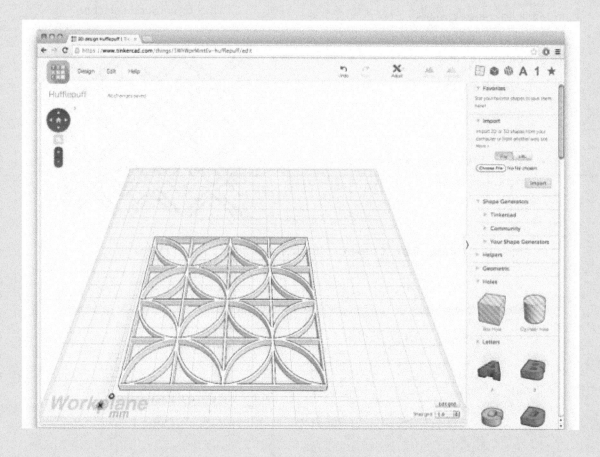

Hardware

All the projects in this book use various hardware, sometimes in combination. This chapter introduces the hardware and supplies you will need to complete these projects.

MaKey Makey

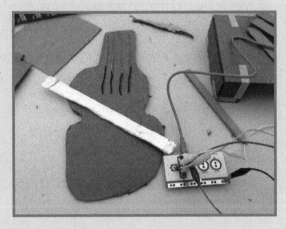

The MaKey MaKey (http://makeymakey.com) is an interface board that, at its simplest, is a keyboard with the left, right, up, down, and spacebar. They include the mouse click for free, too.

The MaKey MaKey allows you to connect anything in the world that is conductive to your computer. When you hold the alligator clipped to the Earth, or ground, port on the MaKey MaKey and touch the conductive object you have also connected to the MaKey MaKey, the MaKey MaKey senses a closed circuit, and passes on the key press to the computer to which the MaKey MaKey is connected. From there, anything you can do on your computer that uses those keys can be touch activated.

The possibilities with the MaKey MaKey are endless, and new inventions using the MaKey MaKey appear regularly. Once you become accustomed to the basics of the MaKey MaKey you can turn it over for access to additional keys as well as mouse movements and additional click functionality.

3D Printers

Access to 3D printers is becoming increasingly more common. Libraries, schools, maker spaces, and even individuals can take advantage of a variety of manufacturers as well as printing materials.

One consideration of 3D printing is the time the model takes to print. With a queue of work waiting to be printed, the task of producing a class or workshop's worth of 3D prints quickly becomes daunting.

Jaymes Dec (http://jaymesdec.com), who leads a Fab Lab at Marymount School in New York City, suggests that a few large format printers coupled with many relatively inexpensive, smaller footprint 3D printers that can produce smaller parts, is one solution to the problem of trying to produce many 3D prints. Another consideration is that perhaps not everybody gets a 3D print. Instead, people collaborate on smaller pieces that when combined form a larger object that can be displayed or placed in a school library for others to "check out" and play with themselves.

LEGO WeDo

The LEGO Education WeDo Construction Set (http://education.lego.com/en-us/lego-educa-tion-product-database/wedo/9580-lego-educa-tion-wedo-construction-set) contains a USB hub, a tilt sensor, a distance sensor, a motor, and assorted bricks and connectors. It allows you to extend your existing LEGO bricks and sets by connecting to your computer and programming Scratch to read the sensors and turn the motor on and off with varying levels of power.

The WeDo hub accommodates the motor and one sensor being connected, or two sensors (but no motor). There is a "hacked" version of the Scratch

Squeak image that allows you to connect two LEGO Power Function motors to the USB hub (https://sites.google.com/site/michaelvorburger/wedo).

PicoBoard

The PicoBoard (http://www.sparkfun.com/products/11888) is a sensor board that includes a microphone, a light sensor, a button, a slider, and four inputs that measure resistance. It can be used with Scratch to allow interaction between the world and your Scratch projects. Currently, Scratch 1.4 is the best version to use with a PicoBoard.

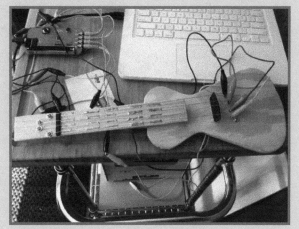

The PicoBoard differs from the MaKey MaKey because it is less "from scratch" than the MaKey MaKey: the button is already built for you, for example. In this way it might allow novice Scratch users to quickly built an interactive project that utilizes one of the sensors on the PicoBoard.

Supplies

Each project in this book has its own list of supplies. Many are readily available around you in the form of recyclables or upcycled materials.

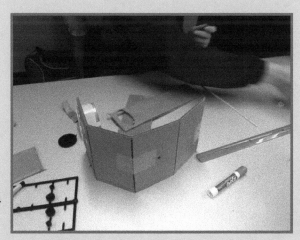

If you keep cardboard, wire, wire strippers/cutters, scissors, copper tape with conductive adhesive, pencils, and rulers on hand, you can easily start many different fun projects. Find new purposes in materials around you, approach your projects with a "make your own" mentality, and you will have fun and learn in the process. I hope these projects are inspiring for you and inspire you to remix, personalize, and expand upon them. Document and share your work and have fun!

Vendors

You can find many of the materials you need at local hardware and craft stores or even Amazon.com. The supplies list for the projects in this book suggest part numbers for some supplies, but you may find better (or cheaper) alternatives elsewhere. Some communities have recycling centers that cater to schools such as the Resource Area for Teaching (RAFT) network (www.raft.net). In addition, the vendors below carry many supplies, excellent learning resources, video tutorials, and best of all, many offer education discounts - be sure to ask!

- Sparkfun - http://sparkfun.com
- Adafruit - http://adafruit.com
- MakerShed - http://makershed.com
- Digi-Key - http://digikey.com

Projects

Squishy Circuit Experiments

Squishy circuits are constructed using homemade conductive and insulating dough (http://courseweb.stthomas.edu/apthomas/SquishyCircuits/). Similar to Play-Doh, the conductive dough can be used to make connections that you would typically use a soldered connection to complete. You can rapidly prototype different types of circuits simply by connecting your components to small blobs of conductive dough.

Challenge Level

The following project is based on a ninety-minute workshop that leads people through building circuits then challenges them to read a circuit diagram to construct a working Operation-type game.

Materials

- Conductive dough (recipe at http://courseweb.stthomas.edu/apthomas/SquishyCircuits/)
- 9v battery with snap connector and leads or
- 4AA batteries with battery holder and leads
- Assorted 5mm or 10mm LEDs
- Piezoelectric buzzer
- 1.5-3V DC motor
- 22 gauge solid hookup wire
- Wire cutters/strippers
- Small box (a macaroni and cheese box works well)

- White paper
- Scissors
- Aluminum foil
- Glue Stick
- Crayons
- Chopsticks
- Small pieces of cardboard to act as insulators and propellers

Optional

- Insulating dough (recipe at http://courseweb.stthomas.edu/apthomas/SquishyCircuits/)
- LEGO bricks to make an organ or bone for the Operation game

Squishy Circuit Experiments

1. Make conductive dough according to the recipe. Optionally, make insulating dough, too.

2. Divide the large ball of conductive dough into smaller balls, one for each participant.

3. Each participant should divide the ball of conductive dough into two balls. Determine the polarity of your LED and put the positive lead in one ball of conductive dough and the negative leads in the other ball of dough.

4. Put the positive lead from your battery pack into the positive ball of conductive dough, and the negative lead into the negative ball. Turn on the battery pack and the LED will illuminate. This type of circuit is called a Parallel Circuit. Continue adding LEDs, noting the polarity of each, to add more light.

5. Disconnect the battery pack from the conductive dough. Disconnect the LEDs from the conductive dough. Make three balls of conductive dough. Arrange the balls in a line, making sure they do not touch.

Some participants might have balls of conductive dough touching. Do not correct this short circuit, but rather when the LED does not light up, have the person separate the balls and note that the LED illuminates: a short circuit demonstrated and corrected!

LEDs have different resistance, depending upon color. If you use the same color LEDs in a parallel circuit they should all be approximately the same brightness. The more LEDs you add to the circuit the bigger load you are putting on the battery, so the intensity of the light will diminish.

6. Connect the positive lead of the battery pack to the leftmost ball of conductive dough. Connect the negative lead of the battery pack to the rightmost ball of conductive dough.

7. Connect the positive LED lead to the positive ball of conductive dough. Connect the negative LED lead to the center ball of conductive dough.

If you were going to design lighting for a parking lot, would a series circuit or a parallel circuit be a better choice to insure consistent, bright lighting?

8. Connect the positive LED lead of a second LED to the center ball of conductive dough. Connect the negative LED lead to the negative ball of conductive dough, the rightmost. This is a Series Circuit.

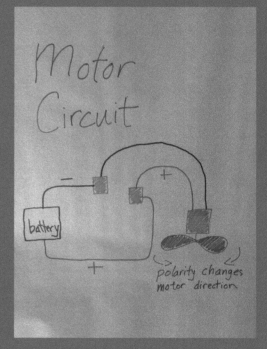

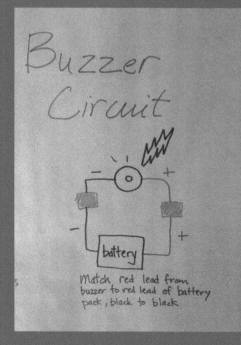

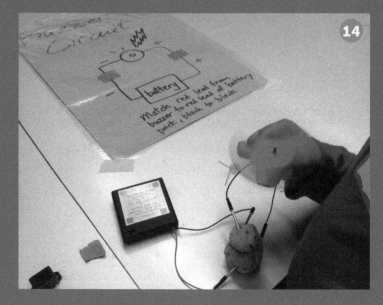

9. You can continue to make more balls of conductive dough and extend the circuit. What happens to the intensity of light from the LEDs the longer the circuit becomes?

10. Disconnect the battery pack from the conductive dough. Disconnect the LEDs from the conductive dough. Make two balls of conductive dough.

11. Cut a small propeller shape from the cardboard. Affix the propeller to the drive shaft on the DC motor.

12. Connect the positive battery lead to one ball of conductive dough. Connect the negative battery lead to one ball of conductive dough.

> Nothing happening? The resistance of the conductive dough combined with the voltage rating on the motor might mean you need more power. Connect another battery pack to the balls of conductive dough, minding the polarity of the leads and the conductive dough. The motor should start spinning.

13. Cut two small pieces of 22 gauge hookup wire. Strip a half inch of insulation from each end of both wires. Connect the wires to the DC motor.

14. Plug one motor wire into the positive conductive dough. Plug the other motor wire into the negative conductive dough. Turn on the battery pack. You are using a parallel circuit to make the motor turn.

15. As the motor spins, note the direction the propeller spins. Turn off the battery pack or packs and disconnect the motor wires from the balls of conductive dough. Reverse the polarity of the motor wires when reconnecting them to the balls of conductive dough: the wire that was in the positive conductive dough is switched to the negative conductive dough, and vice versa. Turn on the battery pack or packs and note the direction the propeller spins.

> Notice how the girl in the motor circuit photo seemingly has one ball of conductive dough sitting on top of the other? This would create a short circuit. But she has used a small scrap of cardboard to insulate between the balls and therefore does not short circuit her parallel circuit.

16. Disconnect the motor from the conductive dough. Connect the positive buzzer lead to the positive conductive dough. Connect the negative buzzer lead to the negative conductive dough. The buzzer makes a sound. You are using a parallel circuit to make the buzzer sound.

17. Disconnect the buzzer wires from the conductive dough.

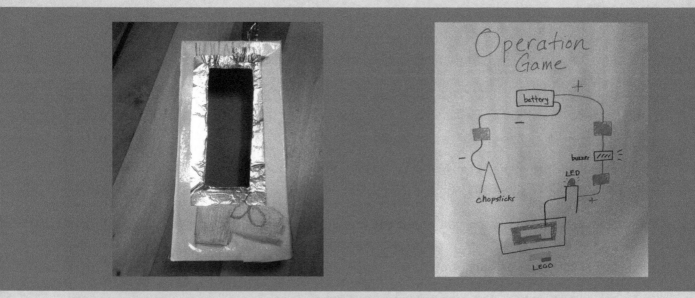

Next, you will use your skills of reading circuit diagrams and building circuits to construct an Operation game.

18. Use the crayons and white paper to outline the shape of your small box.

19. Use the crayons to draw a limb, torso, or head of a person. Cut out the box shape from the paper. Use the glue stick to glue the drawing to one side of the small box.

20. Use the scissors to cut a small hole in the box. The hole will be where you are plucking a bone or organ from the patient, so it needs to be large enough to fit both the object and the chopsticks you use to remove the object.

21. Line the edge of the box hole with aluminum foil, gluing it to the box with the glue stick. Before you completely glue the foil to the box, bend the leads on an LED so the LED will sit flat against the box. Glue the negative LED lead under the aluminum foil.

22. Cut a thin strip of aluminum foil. Use the glue stick to glue this strip of foil over the positive LED lead. Your squishy circuit Operation game box is built.

23. Cut two two foot long lengths of 22 gauge hookup wire. Strip insulation from the last eight inches of one end of both wires. Strip half an inch of insulation from the other end of both wires.

24. Loosely coil the stripped end of the wire up the chopsticks.Use a LEGO brick or a piece of conductive dough to make an organ or bone for your Operation game box. Test with the chopsticks to make sure you can remove the organ or bone with a little effort.

25. Use the circuit diagram to construct your Operation game using the game box from step 21, the chopsticks, and the buzzer. Properly constructed the LED will illuminate and the buzzer will sound if the chopsticks make contact with the foil and complete the circuit.

Things to try

1. Try building a circuit that contains all the components you worked with: LEDs, a buzzer, and a motor. Use small scraps of cardboard if you need insulators. You might need additional power supplies, too.

2. Use a buzzer circuit to do something other than annoy people around you. Can you use a short circuit to make a song? Does changing the size of the conductive dough balls alter the pitch of the buzzer?

3. Develop a set of rules for your Operation game. How many times does lighting the LED and buzzing the buzzer mean your turn is over?

4. Use some hookup wire connected to an LED. Put the LED inside a balloon then inflate and tie shut the balloon. Put the hookup wire into a parallel circuit of conductive dough with a power supply. Does squishing the conductive dough affect the resistance in the circuit and change the intensity of the LED illumination?

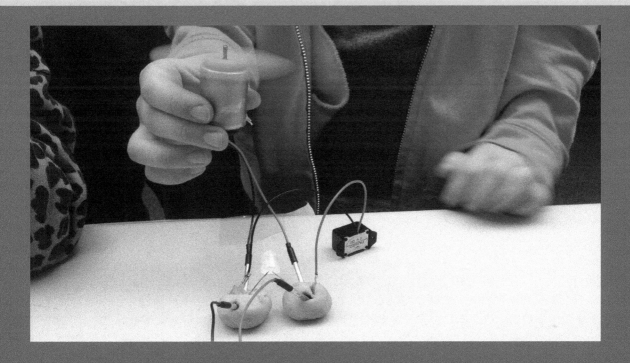

LEGO ArtBots

The LEGO WeDo kit is an excellent construction kit to build simple robots that help you create art. The kit includes a motor, a tilt sensor, a distance sensor, and a USB hub that allows you to connect your ArtBot to a computer to program it in Scratch. Of course, you may supplement the WeDo kit with your own LEGO collection. This project will not lead you through a build of an ArtBot step by step. Rather, it will explore different build techniques that utilize the LEGO WeDo parts that can be creatively used in many different ArtBots. The programs control some of these ArtBots, while others rely on the robot's movement and randomness to generate their art.

Challenge Level

Many of these ArtBots are quite simple to build and were created by fourth graders. Other ArtBot models are a little more complex. This is a medium difficulty project.

Materials

- LEGO WeDo Kit
- Computer running Scratch
- Dry erase markers
- Marking pens for paper
- Masking tape
- Large sheets of paper
- Whiteboard
- Scissors, string, and rubber bands

Optional materials

- Additional LEGO bricks
- LEGO Power Functions extension cables
  (http://shop.lego.com/en-US/)LEGO-Power-Functions-Extension-Wire-20-8871)
- Camera

How the ArtBot Holds Its Pen

Here are two ways you can build your ArtBot to hold a pen. Both work on wheeled vehicles as well as more unusual configurations.

One way for the ArtBot to hold its pen is to construct the pen into the body of the robot itself. By building a small box of LEGO around the marking pen, you can build a penholder that can be incorporated into many different ArtBot designs. You can use bricks or plates to construct your captured pen model. The ArtBot can then push or pull the pen across the drawing surface.

Another way for the ArtBot to hold the pen is attached by rubber bands to a vertical arm. Use the black pegs to attach the pen and holder to the side of a vehicle.

LEGO WeDo is controlled by the programming language Scratch on the computer. Program a loop that switches between turning the motor "this way" and "that way" and running the motor for a couple of seconds, depending on the size of the paper you use. Use masking tape to tape down the corners of your paper so it does not move under the ArtBot as the ArtBot drives around on the paper.

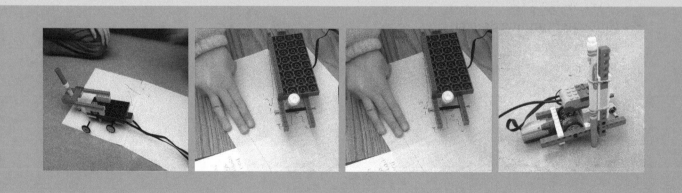

Whiteboard Crawler ArtBots

A large whiteboard, like those found in many school classrooms, makes a great canvas for your ArtBot to explore. If the whiteboard has a pen tray at the base you can build ArtBots that are wheeled and travel back and forth along the pen tray. Make sure you photograph or take video of the work because it only lasts until somebody erases the whiteboard. A simple whiteboard ArtBot used a cam attached to an arm. The arm and cam were attached to an ArtBot that had a

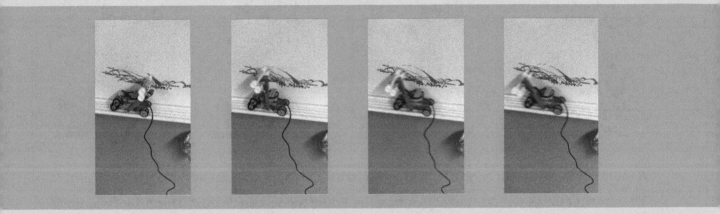

gear train that came in contact with the cam. Because of the irregular shape of the cam, the arm would jump unpredictably. Attaching a dry erase marker or two to the arm allowed the ArtBot to draw on the whiteboard.

The whiteboard ArtBot below used a jointed arm to make the back and forth motion along the pen tray translate into an unpredictable but circular pen stroke.

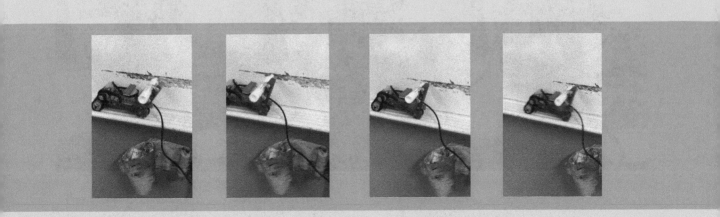

Another whiteboard ArtBot prototype included a tall tower. A free-swinging weight on an arm was suspended in the tower and allowed to swing back and forth. Dry erase markers were attached to the swinging arm with rubber bands. The swinging weight affected the travel of the ArtBot, too, building more randomness into its pen stroke.

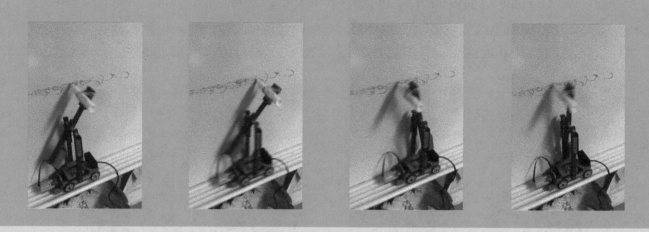

A more advanced ArtBot might include a gear train. The gear train can raise and lower an arm. The stronger the gear train, the more robust the ArtBot model can be built. This ArtBot was built to drive along the pen tray on a whiteboard.

The arm moved up and down through a good range without running the motor long enough for the arm to fall out of the model.

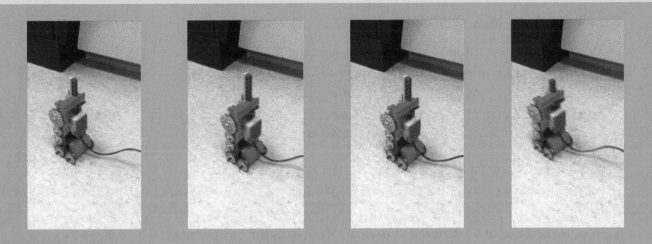

The only problem with this ArtBot was it was so large it did not easily fit in the pen tray and would frequently fall to the floor! Time to go back to iterating on this ArtBot to make it more compact without sacrificing the robust features of the design.

A final whiteboard ArtBot loses wheels and uses a counterbalance and spool to create beautiful, sweeping arcs on a whiteboard or on a large piece of paper mounted on a wall. Additionally, it uses the tilt sensor to provide interactivity between the viewer/user and the ArtBot.

How to Make A Mounted ArtBot

1. Stack and connect three 2X8 plates. In the center peg hole on your new plate brick, insert the WeDo peg that has a cross connector on one end and a circular "hold fast" connector on the other end. Place a crown gear, teeth facing out, on the cross connector. Use masking tape to attach the crown gear assembly to the whiteboard.

2. Use bricks to create a medium sized counterbalance weight. By designing the weight model as a flat stack of bricks the weight will stay against the whiteboard well, which helps keep the pen on the board, too. Tie one end of the string to the weight. Drape the string behind the crown gear assembly taped to the whiteboard so the weight hangs below the assembly.

3. Construct a penholder. A penholder that incorporates the pen into the model works particularly well because it allows you to adjust where the holder sits along the length of the pen. This can be helpful to get a good angle of the pen on the board to produce the best pen stroke.

4. This penholder used bricks, axles, bushings, a plate, and rubber bands to hold the pen securely.

5. Attach the penholder to the string draped behind the crown gear at a distance down the string length to allow for a wide amount of arc movement.

6. The grey WeDo base plate serves as a great platform to build the spool system. Use the motor with a medium size axle. Two of the green WeDo wheels inserted on the axle serve as a spool. Make sure to space the wheels to allow enough string to be reeled in without spilling out of the spool. You will need to mount the motor perpendicular to the base plate. You can build a small platform on which the motor sits then use two of the red WeDo parts pictured here.

7. Use bricks that have holes in them positioned side by side for the motor platform. Put a small black connecting peg in the last hole of the bricks, one on each side, facing out. Use two of the red WeDo parts,

pictured under the motor closest to the grey base plate, to attached the motor platform to the base plate by attaching the red parts to the black connector pegs. Attach the red parts to the grey base plate. The USB hub can also be mounted on the base plate. Plug the motor into the USB hub. Tape the grey base plate to the whiteboard at the same height as the crown gear assembly but spaced about three feet apart.

8. Tie the end of the string to the axle in the middle of the spool.

9. If you have a Power Functions Extension Wire attach it to the USB hub. Attach the tilt sensor to the extension wire. Otherwise, attach the tilt sensor directly to the USB hub. Attaching the tilt sensor to a small base makes it easier to properly orient the sensor for the Scratch program and easier to hold.

10. The WeDo tilt sensor reports five values. Hold the tilt sensor so the cable points at you.

    -   Not tilted = 0
    -   Tilted away from you = 1
    -   Tilted to the right = 2
    -   Tilted toward you = 3
    -   Tilted to the left = 4

11. Program Scratch to change the direction of the motor when the tilt sensor reports either 1 or 3. Stop the motor when the tilt sensor reports 0. As the motor reels in string onto the ArtBot's spool, the penholder is pulled in an arc. As the motor lets out string the penholder swings back along an arc, pulled by gravity. The counterweight can be adjusted to move the position of the penholder on the whiteboard.

Paper ArtBots

ArtBots that draw on paper use the same construction techniques as the whiteboard ArtBots. They often hold a pen perpendicular to the drawing surface. Try a single ArtBot on a sheet of paper and see what patterns emerge. Taping a large sheet of paper to the floor lets several ArtBots explore the canvas and will create interesting art.

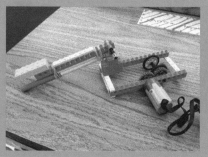

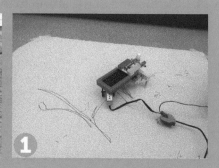

A simple paper ArtBot is a vehicle that travels back and forth in a straight line on the paper. The vehicle can be lifted up and set back down on a different part of the paper to build a pattern as the ArtBot runs its Scratch program. The Scratch program is a looping procedure that sets the motor's direction to "this way," runs the motor for a couple seconds depending on the size of the paper, then sets the motor direction to "that way" and runs the motor for a couple of seconds.

1. By adding a steerable wheel assembly to a vehicle model you can add either an element of control for the ArtBot's user or build in randomness to the ArtBots movements.

2. An ArtBot programmed to run back and forth that includes a rotating front wheel assembly will move in an unpredictable manner.

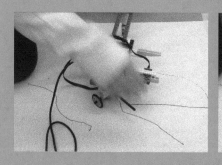

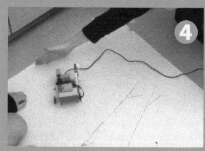

3. A steerable ArtBot includes a rotating front wheel assembly and a long axle to use as a rudder.

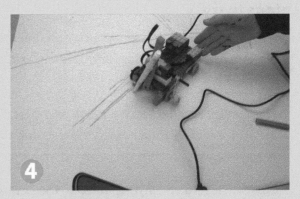

4. Incorporating the distance sensor into the ArtBot's design allows Scratch to read how far the ArtBot is from another object. The ArtBot user can then "paint" using the ArtBot by using her or his hand to interact with the distance sensor. A Scratch program that reverses the motor direction depending on what the distance sensor reports can make the ArtBot reverse when the user's hand gets close to the sensor, pushing the pen along. When the user's hand gets far from the distance sensor, the ArtBot reverses direction again.

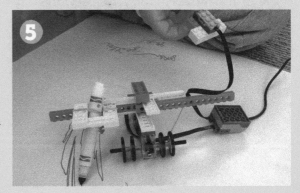

5. Similarly, a tilt sensor can control the ArtBot.

6. Finally, here is an ArtBot model that uses the distance sensor. As the viewer approaches the ArtBot and its distance sensor, the ArtBot extends its arm, holding a pen, toward the viewer.

7. Additionally, through the use of the WeDo gearbox, a second arm moves up and down as the first arm extends and retracts. This drags the ArtBot in an unpredictable way around the drawing surface.

Things to try

1. Because of the limitless ways you can construct LEGO vehicles, experiment with incorporating the sensors, motor, and a pen assembly into vehicles that travel fast, slowly, in regular and irregular patterns or distances.

2. Build an ArtBot that holds a brush and uses paint. The wheels will create a secondary pattern as they roll over wet paint. What other art supplies can the ArtBot hold? Try crayons, pastels, and sponges with paint. Experiment with different mediums.

3. Program a Scratch sprite to include the pen blocks and to make movements on the screen as the ArtBot moves in the physical world. Try to make your on screen art mimic the physical art the ArtBot creates by using creative coding.

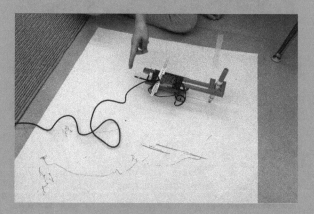

Animated Postcards

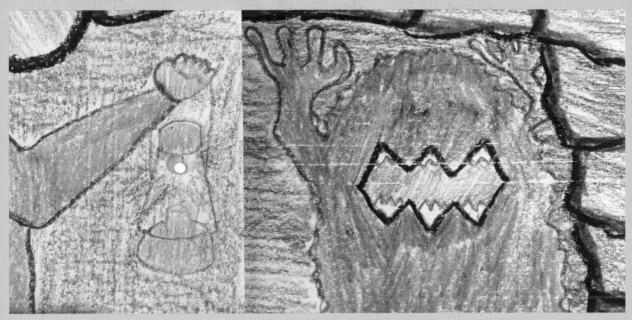

Building on the paper circuits first popularized and elevated to an art form unto themselves by Jie Qi (http://highlowtech.org/?p=2505), this project uses a simple circuit constructed on an index card using copper tape with conductive adhesive, an LED, and a coin battery. The length of your animation is determined only by how many stills you can draw. Imagine something that produces a light: it could be a flashlight, a star in the sky, or a train. Next, imagine what is illuminated as the light approaches or recedes. Combine your circuit and LED with an array of scenes and you can film an animated movie on your smartphone or tablet.

Materials

- 3" x 5" blank index cards
- As many 5" x 7" blank index cards as you want "cells" in your animation
- About 30 cm of copper tape with conductive adhesive (http://amzn.to/1Fm4sMq)
- 5mm LED in the color of your choice

- 3V coin battery CR2032
- 1/4" binder clip
- Plastic coated paperclip
- Markers, red and black
- Pencil and crayons
- Hole punch

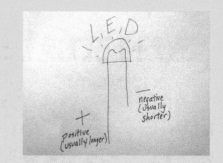

Optional

- Smartphone
- Vine app (vine.co)
- Tablet
- Stop-motion animation software

Challenge Level

This is an easy project. It scales anywhere from first grade to adults.

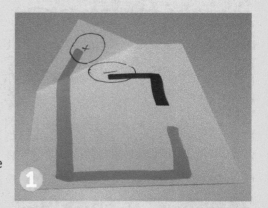

How To Make Animated Postcards

1. On one index card draw a circuit diagram using the red and black marker, red for the positive lead and black for the negative. Your first postcard should be a simple circuit with one LED. Leave a gap between the red lead and the black lead where you will place your LED. Dog ear one corner of the index card where the battery will be placed. It is helpful to remove the battery from its packaging and use it to trace the shape.

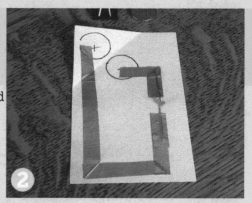

2. Use the copper tape with conductive adhesive to cover the red and black leads with conductive material. Do not cut the tape at the 90 degree bends, but rather fold the copper tape to maintain continuity and conductivity. Make sure you leave a gap for the LED.

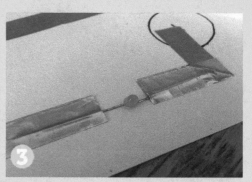

3. Note the polarity of the LED and mark the positive lead with the red marker. Bend the leads so the LED will sit flat against the card. Secure the LED leads to the circuit by sandwiching them between the copper tape on the card and a second, short piece of copper tape.

4. Test your circuit. With a 3V battery correctly inserted into the circuit, with the + side touching the folded-over positive side of the circuit and the underside of the battery sitting on the negative side of the circuit, your LED should illuminate.

> If your circuit does not light up the LED, check for bad connections by running your finger over the copper tape connections sandwiching the LED leads. Make certain you did not reverse the polarity of the LED in the circuit. Make sure that the battery actually works by trying a different battery.

5. Remove the battery from the circuit and set it aside.

6. Spend a few minutes thinking of a creative light source. While a lightbulb immediately comes to mind, take the time to come up with a light source that might be found in an interesting location, or might illuminate something interesting when turned on.

7. Paperclip a blank 3" x 5" index card over the circuit card. Use a very light colored crayon to mark where the LED is on the circuit on the card attached in front of the circuit. Remove the circuit card and paperclip and set aside. Use a pencil to sketch your object that is casting light.

8. Use your crayons to completely color the object and card. Use a hole punch to remove a small hole through which the LED fits.

9. Insert the battery in the circuit. Use the binder clip to hold the battery in place. Use the paperclip to hold the colored index card in front of the circuit index card and LED.

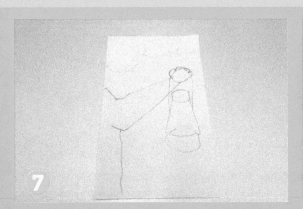

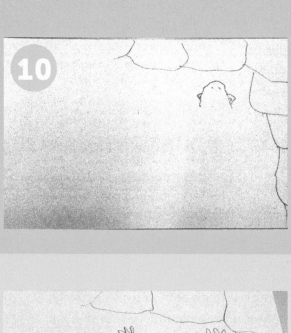

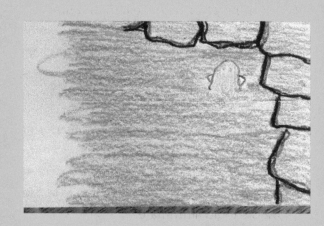

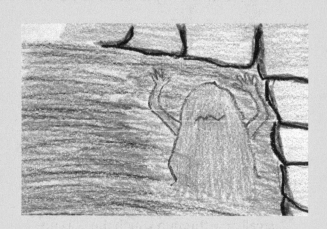

10. Place your illuminated circuit and drawing on a 5" x 7" index card. What is the light illuminating? Is there somebody (or something) else coming closer to the light, or fleeing from it? For each "cell" in your animation, first sketch with pencil then color the scene being illuminated by the light. Remove the battery from the circuit while you work.

11. Attach the battery to your circuit. Attach your circuit card and drawing card to the first background card. You can use an app like Vine to create short looping animations by filming short clips of your circuit and light cards in front of each background card in succession. Here are the cards animated in Vine: https://vine.co/v/MQaZg7TpIjA

Things to try

1. Create more frames. While a Vine video is six seconds long, there are an infinite number of slices in those six seconds.

2. Create a more advance circuit. Switches can help animate the LEDs by illuminating different LEDs for each cell or cells that you are swapping into the scene.

3. Create a way to turn this project into a flipbook that could be animated real-time by the person holding your circuit and background cards.

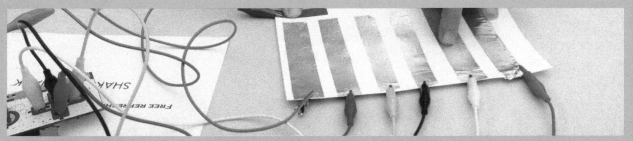

MaKey MaKey Musical Instruments

The MaKey MaKey is the perfect piece of hardware to help you construct musical instruments. No longer do you need to be a luthier to build a guitar. By connecting your home-made instrument to a computer with a MaKey MaKey, you can use Scratch to "program" your instrument to make different sounds. Create a realistic instrument, or dream up an entirely new way to play sounds. These projects are intended as inspirational starting points for your own instruments. The first project, string instruments, introduces many techniques, so if you intend to try a pad instrument as your first project, please read the string instrument section beforehand.

Challenge Level

The MaKey MaKey is simple to use yet provides endless opportunities for exploration in both software and hardware. The challenges provided in these projects are mostly in building the interesting musical interface elements.

Materials

- MaKey MaKey
- Computer running Scratch
- Aluminum foil
- Double-sided conductive copper tape (http://amzn.com/B000UZ8SJK)
- 22 gauge solid hookup wire

- Wire cutters/strippers
- Utility knife
- Scissors
- 5" x 7" index cards
- Cardboard boxes and tubes
- Glue stick and masking tape
- Hot glue gun and hot glue sticks
- Chopstick
- Awl, like on a Leatherman tool

Optional

- Egg carton
- Clothespin
- Heavy gauge wire
- Nuts, bolts, and washers
- Drill
- Crayons & markers
- Pipe cleaners
- 3D printer

Piano Instruments

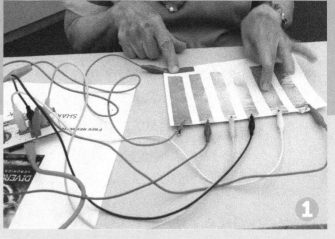

1. For a quick-to-build piano, use an index card and aluminum foil cut into key-sized shapes. Use a glue stick to glue the foil to the index card, making sure the foil extends to the "rear" edge of the note card so you can later attach it to the MaKey MaKey. Additionally, make sure the keys do not touch one another. Add an additional aluminum foil key to the bottom of the piano, the edge of the notecard closest to you.

2. Connect the MaKey MaKey to the computer. Connect the alligator clips to the up, down, left, right, space bar, and the click ports on the MaKey MaKey. Connect an alligator clip to one of the ground, marked "Earth" on the MaKey MaKey, ports.

3. Connect the other end of the alligator clips to the aluminum foil keys on the piano. Connect the Earth alligator clip to the small aluminum foil key at the bottom of the piano.

4. On the computer, use Scratch to program the sound each key should make. Scratch includes a piano keyboard as part of the note selection block to help you easily program a piano keyboard.

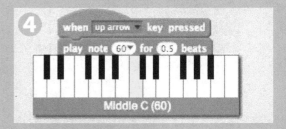

5. With one finger on the Earth key on your piano, you can touch the other keys to play the piano sound you assigned each key.

6. A more durable quick piano can be built in the same manner but replaces the aluminum foil with conductive copper tape.

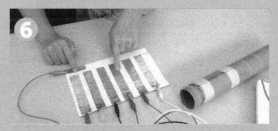

7. Sometimes you find a box that is perfect for a fancy piano. Using the same steps, the box can be transformed into a more durable and perfor-mance-ready piano.

8. A little decorating can bring out the creativity of the MaKey MaKey and Scratch piano you build.

9. An egg carton is a ready-made organ or synthe-sizer keyboard. Separate the two halves of the egg carton. Turn the egg carton pieces over. The side that held the eggs will serve as the keys.

10. Cut pieces of conductive copper tape slightly longer than the keys. Adhere the tape to the egg carton, then fold the tape back on itself to make a small tab. Continue with the remaining cups.

11. Because there are twelve keys on the egg carton keyboard you need to use the back of the MaKey MaKey. Turn the MaKey MaKey over. Use the short wires that come with the MaKey MaKey to connect to the W A S D F G ports on the back of the MaKey MaKey. Use alligator clips to clip to the short wires from the MaKey MaKey. You

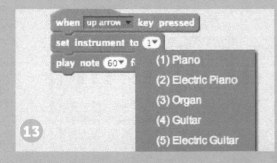

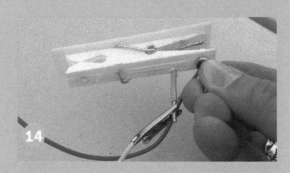

This prototype also used a 3D printed key to make it more realistic. A thin bead of hot glue affixed the ABS piano key to the clothespin.

may also use the arrow keys, space bar, and the click on the MaKey MaKey.

12. Connect the other end of the alligator clips to the copper tape pads on the egg carton keyboard.

13. In Scratch, use the "set instrument" block to choose an organ sound (or any other instrument you want your keyboard to make).

14. Heavy-duty piano keys can be constructed using clothespins, heavy gauge wire, nuts, bolts, and washers. Cut a short piece of heavy gauge wire and strip insulation from each end. Bend the wire at the half point into a 90 degree bend.

15. Drill a hole through the clothespin near where the spring holds the halves together. Drill other hole on the same half, this time towards the end where the two halves meet.

16. Insert the bent wire through the hole near the spring. Secure it to the top half of the clothespin with hot glue.

17. Insert a bolt through the other hole. Secure the bolt to the clothespin with washers and nuts.

18. Connect an alligator clip wire to the heavy gauge wire. Connect the other end to one of the Earth ports on the MaKey MaKey.

19. Clip another alligator clip wire to the bolt. Connect the other end to one of the keys on the MaKey MaKey.

Stringed Instruments

1. Draw your stringed instrument on a sheet of cardboard. Use a utility knife to cut it out.

2. A realistic stringed instrument, like a guitar or violin, can be constructed using lengths of solid hookup wire with the insulation stripped. For this example we will build a four-stringed instrument. Cut four equal lengths of solid hookup wire.

3. Use the wire strippers to remove small sections of insulation from one end of each wire. Continue removing insulation until you have exposed enough of the wire that you can comfortably touch the wire along the length of the instrument's body or neck, depending on how you will play the instrument.

4. Poke holes in the neck and body of the instrument. Push the wires through the holes and secure with hot glue.

5. Another way elevates the strings from the body of the instrument. Cut two small "bridges" from cardboard. Use an awl to punch four holes in each bridge to string the wire through. Use hot glue to attach the bridges to the top of the neck of the instrument as well as towards the base of the body.

6. String the instrument by putting the wire through the holes in the bridge. Secure the wires with small blobs of hot glue.

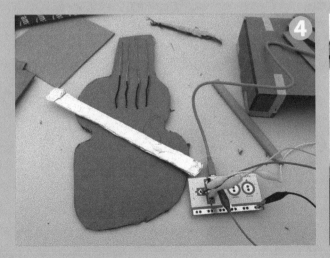
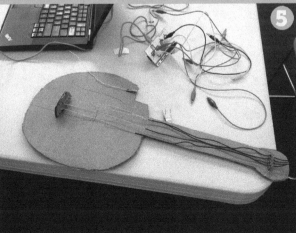

7. If your instrument is played with a pick, you can use a small piece of cardboard covered in aluminum foil or conductive copper tape as the ground for your instrument. Connect an alligator clip wire to the pick. Connect the other end of the alligator clip wire to the Earth port on the MaKey MaKey.

8. Program Scratch to set the instrument to a guitar sound. Program each of the arrow keys for the MaKey MaKey.

9. Connect an alligator clip wire to each of the four guitar strings. Connect the other end of the alligator clip wire to the appropriate arrow key on the MaKey MaKey.

10. When you touch the strings with the pick the computer will play a guitar note for you. You can also hold the pick in one hand and touch the strings with another since you will still be grounded to the MaKey MaKey.

11. If your instrument is played with a bow, cut a piece of cardboard into a bow shape. Cover the cardboard with aluminum foil or with a strip of conductive copper tape.

12. Another approach to building a stringed instrument is to use thin strips of conductive copper tape in place of the wire.

13. Cutting a cardboard tube in half on its circumference makes the copper tape strings easier to bow.

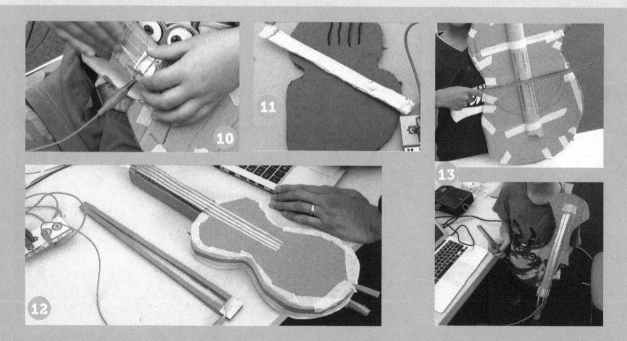

14. By tracing the shape of the instrument's body onto another sheet of cardboard, you can construct a more durable and solid stringed instrument. Cut lengths of cardboard the width of which determines how thick the instrument is. Use hot glue and masking tape to attach the strips to the edge of the bottom side of the instrument.

15. Secure the top side of the instrument to the bottom with hot glue and masking tape.

Pad Instruments

Pad instruments use small pads of aluminum foil, conductive copper tape, and solid core hookup wire to provide conductive points that can be connected to the MaKey MaKey.

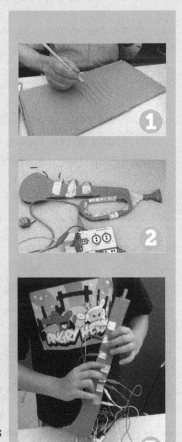

1. The valves of a trumpet can be replaced with pads. Draw a trumpet shape on a piece of cardboard. Use a utility knife to cut it out.

2. Use conductive copper tape pads for each of the trumpet's valves. A thoughtfully positioned conductive copper tape pad can serve as the ground and allow you to play the trumpet one-handed.

3. An oboe can be constructed similarly with copper tape pads.

4. Drums can be made from aluminum foil and wire pads. Trim an 18 inch piece of solid core hookup wire. Strip about six inches of insulation from one end and about half an inch of insulation from the other end.

5. Shape the uninsulated length of wire into an interesting shape. Squares are boring, circles are somewhat interesting, a spiral is compelling!

6. Cut a piece of aluminum foil into an equally interesting shape.

7. Use masking tape to secure part of the insulated wire segment to the cardboard.

8. Use a glue stick to glue the foil over the bent uninsulated wire. You can clip an alligator clip wire to the other end of the wire to connect it to the MaKey MaKey.

9. Cut a second 18 inch length of solid core hookup wire. Strip about six inches of insulation from one end and half an inch of insulation from the other end.

10. Gently wind the uninsulated length of the wire around a chopstick, starting at the base and working your way up the chopstick. Secure the wire to the chopstick with a piece of masking tape. Connect an alligator clip wire to the chopstick wire. Connect the other end of the alligator clip wire to the Earth port on the MaKey MaKey.

11. Cover the end of the chopstick with a ball of aluminum foil.

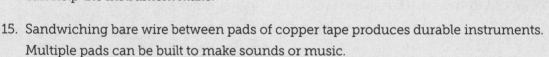

12. Program Scratch to give each pad a different sound, beat, or note when the mallet touches the foil pads.

13. Conductive copper tape can be used in place of foil.

14. Using a coffee container or a similar, lidded container makes the instrument percussive in addition to the sounds the MaKey MaKey can help the instrument make.

15. Sandwiching bare wire between pads of copper tape produces durable instruments. Multiple pads can be built to make sounds or music.

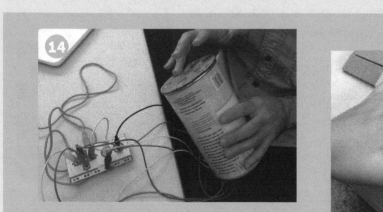

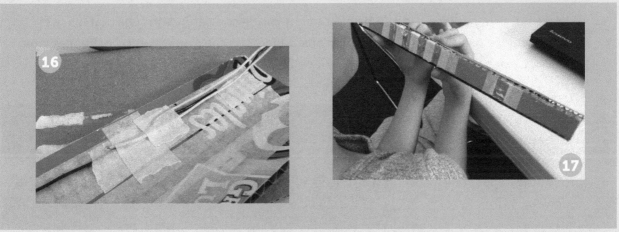

16. By putting holes through the lower layer of conductive copper tape and the cardboard, the wiring can be hidden inside the instruments. Remember to label the wires to help keep track of which wire works with each pad.

17. The resulting flute was programmed in Scratch. Each pad produced a different verse of an instrumental piece that the maker composed and programmed. An additional pad, carefully placed, served as the ground while the flute was held.

18. A trombone can also be built using the wire and copper pad method. Drill holes in a heavy cardboard tube to route the wires.

19. Strip about three quarters of an inch of insulation from a length of solid hookup wire. The cardboard tubes you use determine the length of the wire you use to build the trombone. Label each wire.

20. Apply a small pad of copper tape over each hole and pierce it to allow access to the holes you drilled in the tube.

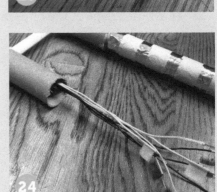

21. Push the wire through the hole, stopping when you reach the uninsulated end pieces.

22. Cover the wire with another piece of copper tape.

23. Use masking tape to even out the diameter of the copper tape pad tube.

24. Feed your labeled wires through the trombone body.

25. A grounding copper tape pad can be built on the inside of a cardboard tube that fits over the copper tape pad tube you previously constructed. Use the same method of copper tape, wire with a small amount of insulation stripped from it, and another piece of copper tape over the wire, this time constructed inside the cardboard tube rather than around it.

26. The finished trombone plays a different trombone note for each copper tape pad the grounding copper tape pad touches.

Unusual Instruments

Instead of creating a MaKey MaKey version of an existing musical instrument, create an entirely new musical instrument. Here is how one young maker built a songbird that would play different pitches of its song and whose wing also produced a beat when the switch behind it was closed.

1. Draw the shape of the bird on cardboard. Omit the lower half of the bird's beak. Use a utility knife to cut it out. Decorate one side of the bird using markers or crayons.

2. Draw the lower half of the beak and a long "finger" connected to it on another piece of cardboard. This beak half will work as a switch that can be moved in three different positions. Cut out the beak switch.

3. Draw the bird's wing on another piece of cardboard. Cut it out and decorate it like you did the bird. Place the bird's wing on its body and gently mark with a pencil where you want it positioned. Remove the wing and use an awl to put two small holes through the bird's body, under where the wing will sit.

4. Cut seven pieces of solid hookup wire in eighteen-inch lengths. Strip a half inch of insulation from each end.

5. Feed one wire through one hole in the bird's body, stopping when you reach the uninsulated end. Secure the wire to the decorated side of the bird's body with a conductive copper tape pad you construct with two pieces of copper tape and the wire.

6. Feed another wire through the second hole in the bird's body, stopping when you reach the uninsulated end.

7. Using a ruler, hold down half an inch of the bird's wing and fold the wing upwards to crease the cardboard.

8. Hot glue the wing to the bird's body. Close the wing to the bird's body and note where it makes contact with the conductive copper tape pad on the bird's body.

9. Use a conductive copper tape and wire pad to secure the second wire passing through the bird's body to the backside of the wing so when the wing is pressed against the bird's body the two pads make contact.

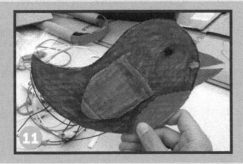

10. Build a conductive copper tape and wire pad on the decorated front side of the beak switch, along the finger, where it will make contact with the back of the bird's body.

11. Using the awl to poke a hole in the bird's beak and in the beak switch. Use a pipe cleaner to secure the beak switch to the bird body.

12. Apply small pieces of conductive copper tape to the back of the bird in an arc that the beak switch can make contact with. Make sure each piece does not touch the next. Place the uninsulated end of the wire on the conductive copper tape pad and secure it with another piece of copper tape. Repeat three times to build a total of four pads.

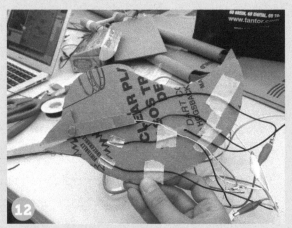

13. Use masking tape to secure the insulated section of each wire to the back of the bird.

14. Connect each wire from the pads to one of the arrow keys on the MaKey MaKey. Connect one wire from the wing to the Space key on the MaKey MaKey.

> You can use the free sound editor Audacity to easily pitch shift a recording you make of your bird's song. Sing or whistle a short tune. Use Audacity to pitch shift it three times, so you have a low to high selection of bird song.

15. Connect the beak switch wire to the Earth port on the MaKey MaKey. Connect the second wing wire to an Earth port on the MaKey MaKey.

16. Use Scratch to program your bird's song. This maker imported a woman's voice that she had pitch-shifted up and down to have four differently pitched versions of the same song. As the beak opened and the beak switch contacted the conductive copper tape pads, the bird would sing, its pitch determined by how open the beak was. The bird's wing used a drum block to play a quiet beat.

Things to try

1. Compose a song that you can play on your instrument.

2. Figure out a way to write down your song so somebody else can play it.

3. Form a band. Rehearse. Perform publicly.

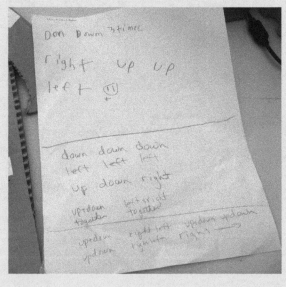

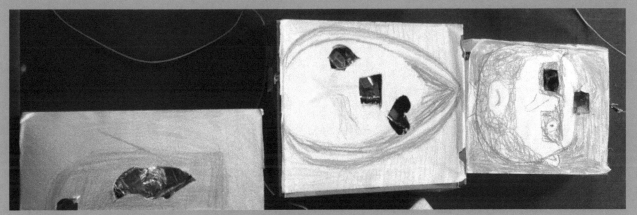

MaKey MaKey Operation Game

You can use a MaKey MaKey, Scratch, and upcycled materials to build your own version of Operation, a classic board game invented in 1965. In the game, the player uses metal tweezers to carefully extract "organs and bones" from the patient without touching the sides of the patient's body. The MaKey MaKey detects these touches and triggers various reactions in the Scratch program. Making your own version of the game allows for infinite variations in the build of the patient and the reactions to success or failure programmed in Scratch.

For example, instead of operating on a human, you could build your own version around a fish and create a biology lesson out of the game. You could code your Scratch program to keep score, add sound effects, or present anatomy facts.

Part of the fun of this project is finding the perfect box to house your game and decorating it. We show a smoked salmon box, but a cereal box works just as well.

Challenge Level

This project has many steps but each is simple. Younger children shoud have help using the X-Acto knife. With practice you can build and program a MaKey Scratch Operation Game in about an hour and a half.

Materials

- MaKey MaKey
- A computer running Scratch
- Alligator Clips
- Chopsticks
- Electrical wire, any small gauge solid wire, like 22 gauge or telephone wire
- Wire cutters/wire strippers
- Cardboard box, like an upcycled cereal box, a box with a nice lid, or even a macaroni and cheese box, plus extra cardboard
- White paper
- Glue Stick
- Scotch tape
- Crayons
- Ruler and scissors
- X-Acto knife
- Aluminum foil
- Hot glue gun and glue sticks
- Playing pieces

Optional

- Double-sided conductive copper tape (http://amzn.com/B000UZ8SJK)

How to Make a MaKey Makey & Scratch Operation Game

1. Choose a box and lay it flat on a piece of white paper. Trace the shape of the box. If you use two straight edges of the paper you only need to trace and cut two sides of the paper. Use the tracing to trim your piece of paper. Set the box aside.

2. Imagine a fun character for your box. Think of a character that is large enough that you can remove objects from it. Use a pencil to rough out your character until you have a design you like. Use crayons to draw the character on the paper. Color it in: you want your design to look better than an off-the-shelf version of Operation.

For the build pictured here, I used a salmon box I had been saving for the right purpose. I saved time because I could use the graphic on the box and modify it just slightly with some new signage. You can use the characters already on a cereal box if you are in a rush to build a version of this game or you doubt your artistic abilities.

3. Use the glue stick to affix the drawing to the front of your box. Make sure you use enough glue that the paper firmly sticks to your box.

4. Use a pencil to gently outline where you are going to cut holes in the character. Keep in mind the holes need to be large enough to contain the object the player tries to remove, as well as the chopstick the player uses. The MaKey MaKey has four arrow keys and a space key, so aim to build at least four holes and up to ten holes (if you use W A S D F G on the back of the MaKey MaKey) in your game box.

5. Use an X-Acto knife to carefully trace the outlined holes. If you go slowly, and don't try to get through all the layers of cardboard at one time you can cut a clean hole. Repeat to cut out the rest of the holes. Keep the cut out parts to use as templates for the rest of your box build.

6. Measure the interior width and depth of your Operation box. Cut a piece of cardboard that is slightly smaller than the width and depth of the box. This piece of cardboard serves as the "motherboard" for your Operation game.

7. Place the motherboard inside the box. With a friend's help, hold the motherboard flush against the top of the box with the holes in it. Trace the holes cut in the box onto the motherboard.

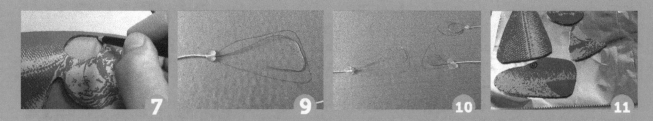

8. Cut lengths of wire long enough to extend from each of the traced holes on the mother-board to beyond the edge of the motherboard: you want extra wire onto which you clip the MaKey MaKey.

9. Strip about three quarters of an inch of insulation from one end of the wire. Strip about three inches of insulation from the other end of the wire.

10. Use the hot glue gun to affix the wire to the motherboard. You just need dots of hot glue over the wire and do not need to use much hot glue. Bend the longer stripped end of the wire to coil around inside the holes traced on the motherboard.

11. Cut pieces of aluminum foil to roughly the same size and shape of each traced hole on the motherboard. You can use your templates from step 5 as a guide. Use a glue stick to affix the foil over each of the wires. Make sure each foil pad is not touching any other pads.

12. Cut as many strips of cardboard as you have holes in your box. The strips of cardboard need to be of equal width so the motherboard will sit flush against the inside top of the box. The wider the strip, the deeper the "cup" on your playing board will be and the more difficult the game will be. Once cut, bend the cardboard into the shape of the hole you traced on the motherboard. The templates from step 5 are helpful for this part. Trim any extra cardboard so you have strips of cardboard fit around the template shapes. Unfold the cardboard strip.

13. Use a glue stick to glue aluminum foil to the cardboard strips. Leave an extra half inch of foil hanging off one side of the strip so the sides of the cup are guaranteed to be in contact with the foil at the bottom of the cup. Cut this strip of foil perpendicular to the strip of cardboard at quarter inch intervals so you can fold the flaps over, inside the formed cup.

14. Use a hot glue gun and hot glue to attach the strips of foil covered cardboard, bent into the shapes of the holes in the box, to the motherboard.

15. If you want to map all the cups to a single key on the MaKey MaKey you can twist the exposed end of wires together. Otherwise, the MaKey MaKey and Scratch can read each cup separately by connecting each wire to a different key on the MaKey MaKey.

16. Slide the motherboard into your box and turn the box upside down, so the tops of the cups are flush with the inside of the box and the holes cut in the box. Measure the distance from the bottom of the motherboard to the inside of the box.

17. Cut strips of cardboard that are the width from step 16. These riser strips will elevate the motherboard inside the box so it sits flush against the inside top of the box. Hot glue the risers to the bottom of the motherboard.

Your MaKey Scratch Operation game box is now built!

Build a set of chopsticks to help you operate

1. Cut two lengths of wire, approximately 12-18 inches long. Strip a few inches of insulation from one end and about three quarters of an inch from the other end.

2. Copper tape with conductive adhesive works great for this step, but if you only have aluminum foil, that will work, too. Cut a small piece of copper tape with conductive adhesive and remove the backing. If you are using foil, cover one side of the foil with glue from your glue stick. Lay the wire down across the adhesive at a diagonal. Lay the chopstick over the wire.

3. Carefully fold the copper tape or foil over the bottom of the chopstick and around the chopstick, making sure you capture the wire between the copper tape and the chopstick. Covering the bottom of the chopstick is important so it is conductive, too. Otherwise you build in a way to cheat at your game. Loosely wind the remaining wire up the chopstick.

4. Repeat with the other chopstick.

Connect your Operation game board to your MaKey MaKey and computer

1. Attach an alligator clip wire from your MaKey MaKey to the wires on your motherboard. For simplicity's sake you can connect all the wires from the motherboard to a single alligator clip. This will map all the "cups" on your motherboard to a single key on the MaKey MaKey.

2. Attach the alligator clip at the other end of the wire from step 1 to one of the keys on the MaKey MaKey: the Space key works well, since it is the default key on the appropriate Event Block in Scratch.

3. Attach both wires from the chopsticks to a single alligator clip wire. Attach the alligator clip at the other end of this wire to one of the Earth connections on the MaKey MaKey.

4. Attach the USB cable from the MaKey MaKey to your computer.

Create a Scratch project to work with your game box and the MaKey MaKey

The MaKey MaKey will look for a circuit to be established when the chopsticks touch the foil cups on your motherboard. Scratch responds to the MaKey MaKey's key press with audio and visual feedback that you are hurting the patient. Open your web brower and navigate to http://scratch.mit.edu.

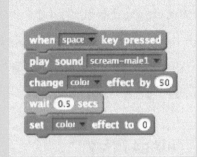

1. Create a new Project.

2. Go to the Events Blocks tab and select the "When space key pressed" block.

3. Go to the Sound Blocks tab and select the "Play sound ___" block. Scratch includes a large library of sounds you can use to indicate that the patient is being hurt.

4. Go to the Looks Blocks tab and select the "Change color effect by 25" block. Also drag a Set color effect to 0 block.

5. Go to the Control Blocks tab and select a "Wait 1 second" block.

6. Connect the blocks to provide an audio and visual feedback to the player when the MaKey MaKey detects a key press. Adapt the code to change how much color effect is applied, and how long the effect displays before being reset.

Play your game!

With the MaKey MaKey connected to the game board, the chopsticks, and your computer, and your Scratch project written, you are nearly ready to play. Add objects that you need to remove from the patient to

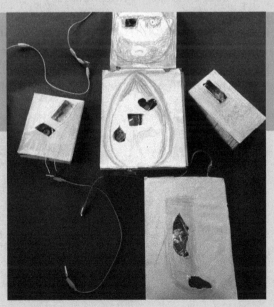

the cups. You can use air-hardening clay, Sugru, LEGO bricks, beads, or anything else you have that resembles the bones and organs in your patient. As you try to remove the objects, keep the chopsticks clear of the aluminum foil cups. If the conductive copper tape and wire on the chopsticks touches the foil Scratch will indicate you are hurting the patient by playing a sound and changing the appearance of the Sprite. I hope your medical malpractice insurance is paid up!

Things to try

1. Build a set of tweezers or modify the chopsticks to be easier to use.

2. Use a 3D printer to design aan print a set of chopstick cheaters that convert them to tweezers.

3. Using Variables in Scratch, create a score keeper mechanism that counts down the number of times you can hurt the patient before the game ends.

4. Use Scratch 2.0's cloud data to keep a running, world-wide "low score" for your game. Lower scores are better.

5. Using Variables in Scratch, build a countdown timer. You have to remove all the items successfully in thirty seconds or the game ends. This addition can compensate for a game board that some find "too easy."

6. Wire the cups to different inputs on the MaKey MaKey and modify your Scratch program to respond to more inputs.

7. 3D print the organs and bones for your patient.

8. Take a photo of your Operation box and use it as the Sprite's Appearance.

Soft Circuit Stuffed Animals

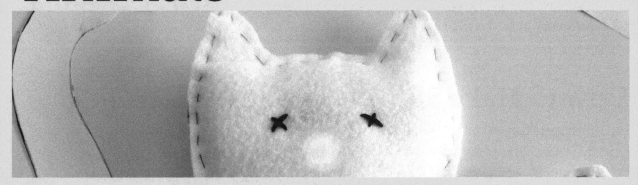

Enliven your stuffed animal collection with a simple-to-sew stuffed animal that includes LEDs that light up. You can give your stuffed animal a personality with glowing eyes, a beating heart, or any other imaginative use of light you can dream up. This project starts with two LEDs but you could sew an army of soft circuit stuffed animals that includes increasingly more complex electronic components.

Challenge Level

With basic sewing skills this project is easy. Some electronic components are small or have fragile connections, so if you are uncertain of your ability ask for help with those parts.

Materials

- 1/3 yard muslin
- 1/3 yard felt, color of your choice (this will be the color of the stuffed animal)
- 1/3 yard batting
- Sewing needles
- Regular sewing thread, color to complement the felt color
- Embroidery thread for stuffed animal features
- Scissors
- Pencil and markers

- Paper
- 5mm blinking red diffused LED (Digi-Key 67-1497-ND)
- 5mm yellow transparent LED (Digi-Key 611-1265-ND)
- Battery holder for 12mm coin cell (Digi-Key BH501-ND)
- CR1225 12mm 3v coin battery
- Conductive Thread, extra thick (SparkFun DEV-10119)
- Needlenose pliers
- Utility knife

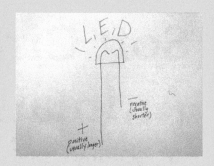

How to Make Soft Circuit Stuffed Animals

1. With a pencil and a clean sheet of drawing paper, sketch out your pattern. You might want to consider making a very simple form for your first stuffed animal if you are just starting sewing. For example, the cat was simplified from standing to sitting.

2. Draw your circuit diagram. There should be one central positive line extending from the battery pack to the positive leads on the LEDs you will use. Additionally, there needs to be a negative line from the negative LED leads. This diagram includes switches, too, though the finished model does not yet incorporate them. You can use the template below as a starting point for exploring soft circuits.

3. Cut out your paper pattern. Trace the pattern onto a piece of muslin. Trace the pattern onto two pieces of felt. Cut out the muslin and felt.

   - The muslin tracing excluded the tail because there is no circuitry in that part of the stuffed animal. You can save time and material on the muslin layer by excluding limbs and other features so long as you leave room for your circuity.

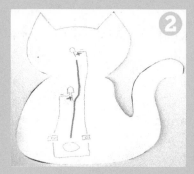
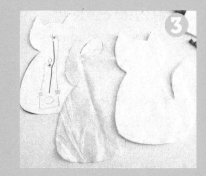

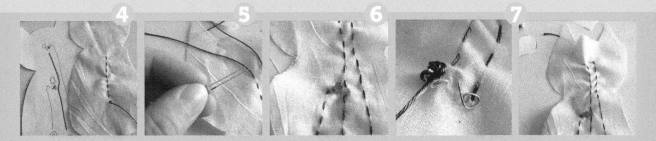

4. Use a pencil to draw the circuit diagram from the paper pattern on the muslin. Stitch the circuitry into the muslin. The extra thick conductive thread requires a needle with a large hole. Also, it does not knot well. However, it is very conductive and great for a novice sewer. When you finish each of the leads leave about five inches of extra conductive thread before you trim the thread so you have thread to connect the components.

5. Determine the polarity of the LEDs you are using. The positive lead is longer. Mark the negative lead with a black marker pen near the LED itself to help you keep the polarity straight.

6. Turn the muslin over so the extra conductive thread side is facing away from you. Minding the polarity of the LED, pierce the muslin fabric with the LED leads and push the LED through until it sits flush with the muslin.

7. Use the needlenose pliers to gently twist the LED leads into spirals to provide a convenient place to connect the conductive thread. Secure the conductive thread "traces" to the LEDs, again minding the polarity of your circuitry.

8. Attach the battery holder to the sewn circuity on the opposite side of the muslin than the LEDs. The battery pack has two pins that are polarized. Make sure the positive pin pierces the muslin near the central positive sewn lead. The negative pin pierces the fabric at some point between the little "bridge" in the circuit diagram, below the battery pack. Use the extra conductive thread on the positive lead sewn circuit to attach to the bent positive pin on the battery holder. Use a short length of conductive thread to sew from the negative pin on the battery holder to the "bridge."

9. Right now there is no switch incorporated into the circuitry. On both negative leads, tie the extra lengths of conductive thread together so they are attached. Minding the polarity, insert a battery into the battery holder. The LEDs should illuminate.

If the LEDs do not light up when the battery is inserted, make sure the polarity on the battery holder is correct and it was sewn into the circuit firmly. Make sure the LEDs are secured to the conductive thread. Check the marking you made on the LED to insure that the the LED leads are connected to the sewn circuit properly. Try a different battery.

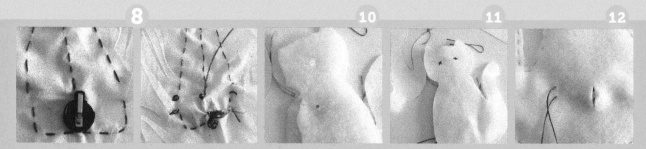

10. Use the paper pattern to cut a piece of batting slightly smaller than the felt cutouts. Poke holes in the batting where it sits over the LEDs so the light is not completely diffused.

11. Use embroidery thread to add features to your stuffed animal.

12. Use the utility knife to cut a small slit in the back piece of felt to provide access to the battery. Thread the extra conductive thread from your sewn circuit onto a needle and pass it through the back piece of felt as well.

13. Use regular sewing thread to sew the layers together: felt with the battery slit on the bottom, the muslin circuit board with electronic components, batting, and the top felt layer with features. When the extra pieces of conductive thread on the back of the stuffed animal are loosely knotted the LEDs will illuminate. This cat's nose glows yellow and its heartbeat, though faint through the felt, gently blinks on and off.

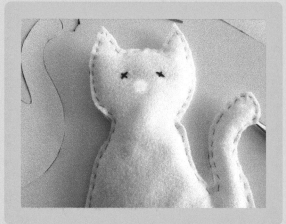

Things to try

1. Incorporate switches into your circuitry. A Radio Shack .5mm High Tact Switch is a good starting point but needs something soldered to the tiny connection tabs to interface with thicker conductive thread.

2. Incorporate the existing extra thread "switch" into part of the stuffed animal's design, so playing with the stuffed animal would cause the LEDs to turn on. The circuity on the cat, for example, could be redesigned so the extra conductive thread used to turn on the circuit was the cat's whiskers.

3. Try using different electronic components. A small vibrating motor added to the circuit and triggered by a switch might make your stuffed animal seem even more lifelike.

TurtleArt Experiments

TurtleArt (http://turtleart.org) is a block-based Logo programming environment. While limited in features compared to other versions of Logo, TurtleArt allows the user to experiment with Logo as an art creation tool. Extremely easy to use, TurtleArt nevertheless is capable of producing art from complex, challenging Logo procedures that you program. What follows is a series of TurtleArt projects that encourage you to consider programming in TurtleArt as an exercise in "building small tools that can make something big," as Dr. Cynthia Solomon described programming in Logo.

Challenge Level

The procedures you will work on range from easy to medium difficulty. TurtleArt scales from elementary age children to adulthood.

Materials

Computer running TurtleArt

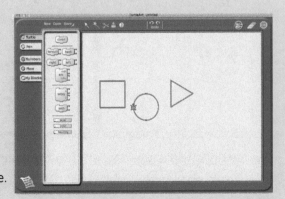

Square, Circle, and Triangle

One way to introduce people new to TurtleArt is to ask them to program a square, a circle, and a triangle.

1. Start with the square. There are many ways to program the turtle to draw a square. There is no one right answer. Some people will put together enough forward and left (or right) blocks that the turtle draws a square. The person might have to click on the blocks multiple times but eventually the turtle will draw a square.

   - Other people might realize that if enough forward and left blocks are put together that the turtle will draw the square in one click of the blocks.

   - The most concise way to program the turtle to draw a square uses the Repeat block. Since a square has four sides, program the turtle to repeat a forward and right (or left) movement four times.

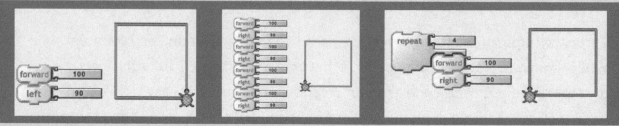

2. The turtle can be programmed to draw a circle in several different ways. First, the Arc block will by default draw half a circle.

   - Changing the angle to 360 degrees will draw a circle in one click of the block.

   - Another way to draw a circle is most apparent if you "put yourself in the turtle's shoes" and walk in a circle while paying attention to your movements. Walking in a circle can be reduced to moving forward and right (or left) at the same gradual interval. Here the turtle is programmed to draw a circle using the Repeat, Forward, and Right blocks.

   - If you want to draw a circle with the turtle in the center of the circle you have you use a few more blocks as well as the Pen Up (pu) and Pen Down (pd) blocks.

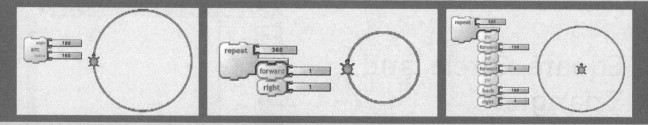

3. Finally, the triangle. Depending upon your knowledge of geometry, this can be a difficult or simple challenge.

Useful rules about triangles

- If you have three equal sides, you will have three equal angles
- If you have two equal sides, you will have two equal angles
- If you have no equal sides, none of the angles will be equal
- The sum of the three angles in a triangle equals 180 degrees

Try drawing these triangles:

- Three equal sides.
- Two equal sides.
- Unequal sides. You can see this is not a perfect triangle but it is a close approximation.

Primatives and procedures

Like other versions of Logo, TurtleArt comes with Primitives, built-in instructions the turtle understands. On the right are the primitives for the turtle's movements.

When you snap together blocks to program the turtle to move and draw, you create a Procedure. You can name your procedure and teach the turtle a new command. Under the My Blocks tab, there is a diamond-shaped block that fits on top of the stack of blocks that make up your new procedure. Click on the diamond block and type a name in the block. Then a corresponding new block will appear in the My Blocks tab and you can use it like any other block.

Using procedures helps make complicated stacks of blocks more efficient, reusable, and easier to read. Procedures can be called within other procedures. They save with your project.

Dr. Cynthia Soloman, one of the inventors of Logo, advised a group of Logo programmers at Constructing Modern Knowledge 2012 that the key to programming in Logo is to build small parts, and use the small parts to build larger parts. Like LEGO, simple elements combine to create complexity.

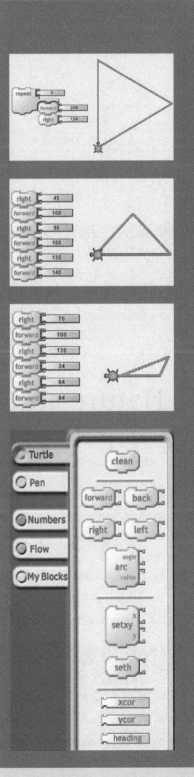

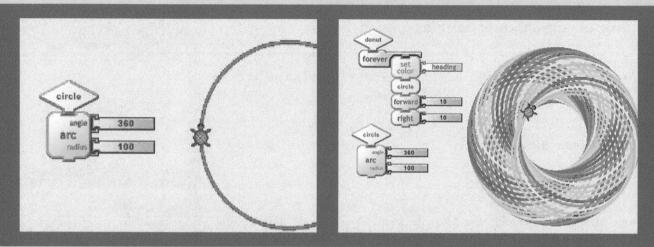

Try this! Write two new procedures: circle and donut

The donut procedure uses the circle procedure. Since the donut procedure uses a forever block, an animation effect is created as the turtle cycles through colors. Use these procedures in a Turtle Art program of your own.

Nature and TurtleArt

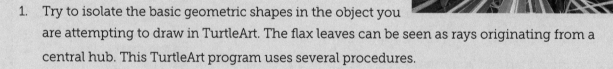

Inspiration for TurtleArt procedures can come from nature. Consider the geometry in this photo of flax.

1. Try to isolate the basic geometric shapes in the object you are attempting to draw in TurtleArt. The flax leaves can be seen as rays originating from a central hub. This TurtleArt program uses several procedures.

2. Try programming your representation using small procedures instead of trying to write a single procedure for the entire drawing. Building randomness into the procedures mimics the variations one sees in nature.

Not all TurtleArt nature procedures need to be this complex. A fall leaf is a simple, fun nature model that scales from TurtleArt to the ProBot, for a real world Logo drawing experience.

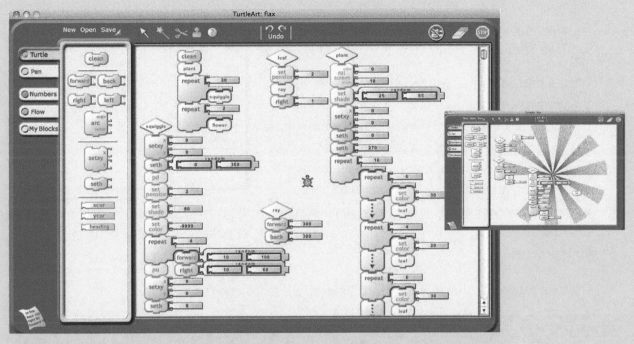

The code for this Turtle Art Flax project is at http://inventtolearn.com/fun/flax

Islamic-Inspired TurtleArt

This project is a good starter for the 3D printed TurtleArt tiles project later in this book. After you work your way through these programming exercises you will understand the math and process of programming a stunning field of geometric shapes.

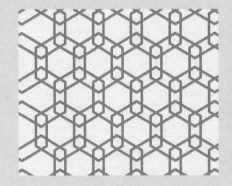

1. Start by programming a new procedure that makes the turtle draw a closed geometric shape. Use the diamond block under the My Blocks tab to name your procedure "hex". An easy way to calculate the number of degrees needed for any polygon with any number of sides is to divide 360 by the number of sides. An octagon would be 360/8 = 45 degrees.

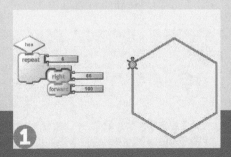

2. By using the SetXY block you can program the turtle to move around the workspace.

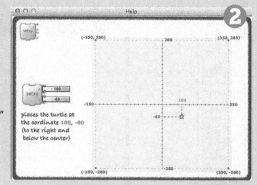

3. Write a procedure that will move the turtle across the workspace from the left to the right drawing hexagons along the way. Name this procedure "horiz." In this procedure the turtle draws a hexagon, moves from its current position on the x-axis 135 steps, and stays on its current y-axis. The hexagons are purposely overlapped because the overlap helps create the pattern. You will have to experiment with your "xcor + number" combination to find the perfect amount of overlap for your procedure.

4. Create a procedure that moves the turtle down the y-axis and name it "vert."

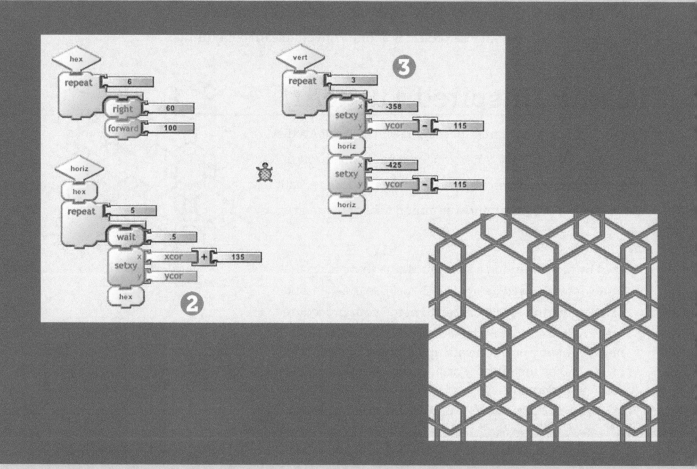

Because every computer screen is different, your procedures will need to be modified in three different places. First, you may have to repeat more than three times to get the turtle's drawings to completely fill your workspace. Second, you will need to change the "setxy" x values for your shape. Third, you will need to customize your "ycor - number" for your geometric shape. Experiment with changing the amount of overlap until you find a beautiful combination of shapes and overlaps that result in new patterns.

5. Write a procedure that fills the entire workspace with overlapping geometric shapes. In this procedure, named "tile", the turtle calls "horiz" and "vert" twice, once with a large pen and a second time with a smaller pen in a different color.

6. Experiment with running the procedure several times with increasingly smaller brushes. This in turn creates new and interesting overlapping shapes.

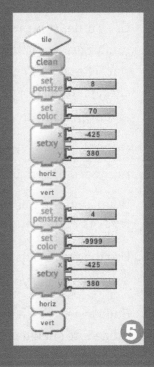

Variable Stars

The next Turtle Art experiment iterates on a star design. It also makes use of the "store in box" block and variables.

1. A star design emerges if you program the turtle to go forward and back the same amount and rotate through 360 degrees.

However, looking at the night sky the stars vary in size, intensity, and color. We want our stars to look more realistic.

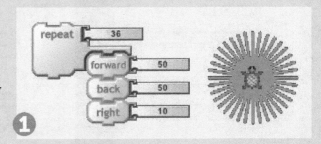

2. Use TurtleArt to program a night sky with stars varying in brightness, color, and the length of lines in each point in the star. The "store in box" block allows you to use variables to change the size of your stars' rays while allowing the forward and back number to remain the same.

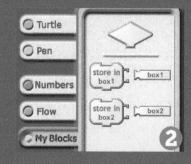

3. Use the "random" number block to generate a random number stored in box1.

4. When you run this procedure the turtle will draw a star with rays of varying lengths.

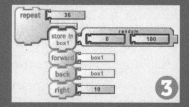

5. Use the small tools you developed to create a field of stars. Start by naming your star procedure.

6. Build a stars procedure that uses the star procedure. This procedure should randomize the shade of the star as well as randomly position the star on the screen.

7. Finally, build a sky procedure that clears the workspace, colors the background, and runs the stars procedure on repeat.

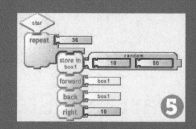

Although this block may seem to be a simple and limited way to handle variables, TurtleArt's "store in box" blocks provide a powerful tool with which to explore the mathematical concepts of variable and variability.

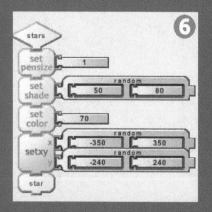

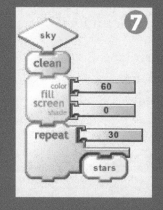

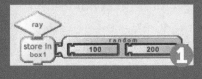

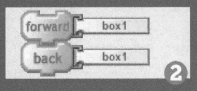

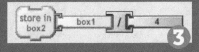

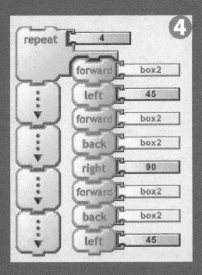

TurtleArt Snowflakes

Another project that builds on Dr. Solomon's recommendation to build small tools that can create larger works is to program snowflakes in TurtleArt. Since no two snowflakes are alike, we can experiment with random numbers again. This time, the snowflake's diameter and the length of the "barbs" along the "arms" will be randomized. Some snowflakes will be larger than others.

1. Create a new procedure by dragging a diamond-shaped block from the My Blocks palette. Name the diamond block "ray." Use the "store in box1" block to help randomize the snowflake's radius.

2. Use a forward and back block with box1 blocks to program the turtle to draw a ray.

3. The barbs along the rays of the snowflake will be one quarter the length of the ray. Store the ray's length divided by four in box2.

4. The barbs are drawn at intervals a quarter of the length of the ray.

5. Reset the turtle to the beginning of the ray it just drew.

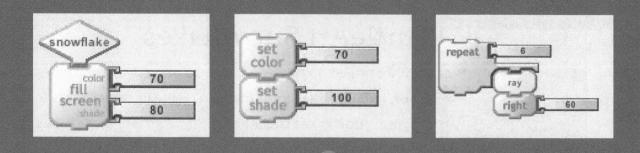

6. Use the ray tool to create a more complex design by incorporating it into another procedure called snowflake. This procedure changes the background color, randomizes the pen size, sets the shade, and draws six-rayed snowflakes. The design of the procedures makes it easy to modify without breaking the functionality.

These TurtleArt procedures should inspire you to continue exploring variable blocks, the store in box1 and box2 blocks. Additionally, you are encouraged to continue programming small tools that used together can produce complex results.

Glowdoodlers

In a famous Life Magazine article photographed by Gjon Mili, Pablo Picasso's brush-strokes are captured in light rather than paint (http://bit.ly/light-picasso). Eric Rosenbaum's Glowdoodle software similarly slows down the exposure on your laptop's camera. The movements you make in front of the camera become smeared, and lights like LEDs or your smartphone's screen leave lasting marks. We will build a couple different electronic light pens, called Glowdoodlers, that you and your friends can use to paint with light.

Challenge Level

These Glowdoodlers are very simple to build as long as you use a ruler and are comfortable using wire cutters to strip wire. The great thing about a Glowdoodler is they can be simple or complex, depending upon your circuit building skills and your access to different tools.

Materials

- Scissors
- Wire strippers
- Hot glue gun and hot glue sticks
- X-Acto knife
- Rubber bands

- Binder clips
- Push pin
- Cardboard
- Wire (any small gauge wire works, though double-strand telephone wire works really well)
- Double-sided conductive copper tape (http://amzn.com/B000UZ8SJK)
- Assorted LEDs
- 3v coin battery, such as a CR2032
- Glowdoodle (http://glowdoodle.com or http://scripts.mit.edu/~eric_r/glowdoodle/)

Optional

- Markers
- Paint
- Computer on which you can install Glowdoodle
- CAD modeling program, such as Tinkercad
- 3D printer

Glowdoodle Software

You can run Glowdoodle in any web browser that can run Java applets. Alternately, you can download and install Glowdoodle on your computer. Take some time to play with Glowdoodle and to understand how the slowed down exposure on the camera affects the images. Try moving different reflective items in front of the camera and see the trails they leave behind. The software you install on your computer allows you to save your work by pressing S on the keyboard. The files are saved in the same directory as Glowdoodle. Once you understand Glowdoodle it is time to build some Glowdoodlers to help you paint with light.

How to Make a Glowdoodler Electronic Paint Brush

There are two Glowdoodler Electronic Paintbrush buiilds in this chapter.

The first Glowdoodler is a slightly more complex build that has the feel of a wand or paintbrush and leaves room for the maker to customize the design. Your paintbrush might have a single LED or a number of LEDs. Test your connections before you glue and make sure the battery is strong enough to light multiple LEDs.

1. Cut a rectangle from medium weight cardboard. Use a ruler to bend the cardboard into a box shape.

2. Run a bead of hot glue from the hot glue gun along a long edge of the cardboard. Fold the cardboard into a box shape and secure it with rubber bands and binder clips while the glue sets.

3. Cut a long strip of cardboard. Fold the strip in half. Mark one side of the cardboard with a + to indicate which side the positive lead on the LED will go.

4. Use a pushpin to poke two holes, parallel to one another, in the fold of the cardboard strip. Poke the LED through the holes, making sure that the positive lead on the LED is on the positive side of the cardboard strip. The positive lead of an LED is slightly longer than the negative.

5. Cut two lengths of wire, slightly longer than the length of the folded cardboard strip and the box you built in steps 1 and 2. Strip the ends of the wire with the wire strippers.

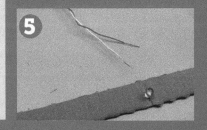

6. Twist one wire around the positive lead of the LED and the other wire around the negative lead. Use a little hot glue to secure the twist and to insulate the connections when the cardboard strip is folded back in half.

7. Use hot glue to secure the LED to the cardboard strip. A little blob of hot glue on the end of an LED, particularly if the LED is bright, can distort and fracture the light in interesting ways.

8. Use a few blobs of hot glue to secure the wires to the inside of the cardboard strip.

9. Fold the cardboard strip in half, wires on the inside. Use hot glue to attach the cardboard strip to the cardboard box. Use binder clips to hold everything together while the glue sets.

10. Next, you are going to build a switch to turn the LED on and off. This photo shows the switch.

11. Cut a piece of cardboard slightly less wide than the box you built and about twice the length of the 3V coin battery. Trace the 3V coin battery in the middle of the piece of cardboard. Use the X-Acto knife to carefully cut a hole in the cardboard where the battery fits, as shown in step 10.

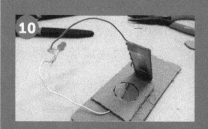

12. Wind one of the wires from the cardboard strip around to the side of the cardboard box you want your on/off switch. Use the wire strippers to remove a little insulation from the end of the wire. Use a couple pieces of copper tape to sandwich the wires between them and secure the tape and wire to the box.

13. Use hot glue to attach the piece of cardboard from step 11 over the piece of copper tape, so the battery will sit in contact with the copper tape and wire.

14. Cut a thin strip of cardboard to glue to the side of the cardboard box with the switch. The other wire can be stripped and similarly held down by pieces of copper tape attached to this cardboard, like in step 10. A more elegant solution is to remove a little more insulation from the wire and twist the exposed wire into a loose coil that can be used to close the circuit and light the LED.

15. When the switch is closed the LED lights up!

16. You can decorate your Electronic Paintbrush with markers or paint. Parts of this paintbrush could be replaced with 3D printed parts. Can you figure out how to wire a circuit that would include multiple LEDs that have individual on/off switches? Can you make a different shaped paintbrush using your skills?

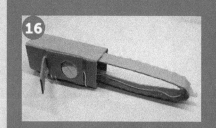

Simple Glowdoodler Electronic Paintbrush

If you need to build many Glowdoodlers for your friends, your classroom, or a workshop then you can use this more streamlined and compact design.

This Glowdoodler Electronic Paintbrush build uses copper tape with conductive adhesive instead of wire, eliminating the need to strip wires. This project also uses a 3D printer to make the battery holder instead of having to carefully cut them out of cardboard. However, you can combine parts of both of these builds as desired.

1. Start by trimming two pieces of cardboard for each Glowdoodler you will build. One piece is approximately 8.5 cm long by 4 cm wide. The other piece is about 7 cm long by 2.5 cm wide. Note the polarity of the LEDs you are using. Secure the negative LED lead to one side of the larger piece of cardboard with copper tape. You get the best conductivity if you first put down a piece of copper tape, then the LED lead, and cover the lead with another piece of copper tape.

2. Use a CAD modeling program such as Tinkercad.com to design 3D printed battery holders. The holders shown in the photo were printed on a MakerBot Replicator 2. (If you don't have a 3D printer, you may also cut them out of cardboard as in the previous build.)

3. Bend the smaller piece of cardboard in half. This will be the switch. Use hot glue to attach it to the back of the larger piece of cardboard.

4. Hot glue the 3D printed battery holder or the cardboard battery holder to the front of the larger piece of cardboard, over the copper tape and negative LED lead.

5. Cut two more strips of copper tape. One should be long enough to reach between the positive LED lead on the back of the cardboard and the flap you glued to the back. The other

strip of copper tape should be long enough to reach between the positive lead strip, around the flap, so it will make contact with the battery when the flap is closed.

6. Cover the positive LED lead with the shorter piece of copper tape. Use the longer piece of copper tape to extend from the positive strip around the flap.

Both Glowdoodlers allow you to easily turn the LED on and off with a switch. You can make single points of light by pointing the LED at the camera and rapidly turning the LED on and off. You can leave long continuous brush strokes by leaving the LED on.

Things to Try

1. Write words in light.

2. Organize a group of people in a dark room to simultaneously turn their Glowdoodlers on and off to create a field of stars. Use the saved Glowdoodle night sky image with a paint program to create your own constellations and creation myths.

3. Although light seems temporary, with Glowdoodle you can capture your ethereal drawings.

4. For a more robust Glowdoodler, the Light Graffiti Cans Instructable is a great build. (http://www.instructables.com/id/Light-Graffiti-Cans-for-Glowdoodle/) This Glowdoodler requires a little soldering but can be more roughly handled by people eager to Glowdoodle.

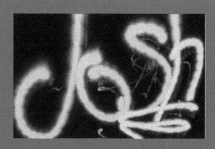

LEGO Chain Reaction Machines

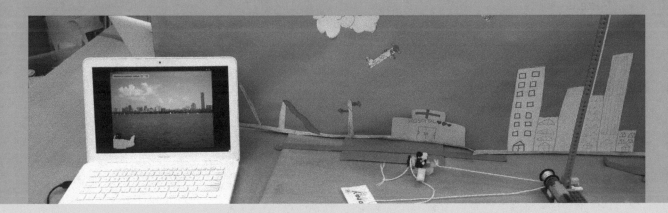

Eric Rosenbaum posted a short YouTube video (http://youtu.be/5mQRQ6vCAwE) that is an amazing prompt for a project that combines engineering, programming, Rube Goldberg's sensibilities, and collaboration to create a wonderful chain reaction machine. As Eric's video demonstrates, you will build a machine that goes from the physical world (using the LEGO WeDo kit's tilt or distance sensors and a motor), into the digital world of Scratch on your laptop, then back into the physical world to trigger the next machine. You can build as long of a chain reaction machine as you have LEGO WeDo kits, laptops, and extra materials.

Challenge Level

Depending on how long your chain reaction machine is, this project is medium to difficult. Each machine requires interaction with the next machine in the chain, so cooperation and collaboration among the group is vital.

Materials

- LEGO WeDo kits, one per each chain reaction machine

- Laptops running Scratch 1.4 or 2 (you will need to install a browser extension to make Scratch 2 work with the LEGO WeDo sensors and motor), one per each chain reaction machine
- Cardboard
- Rulers
- Pencils
- Box cutter knife
- Blue painters tape
- Large work surface where the project can remain over the course of the build, or large pieces of cardboard that the machines can be built on and taped to so the project can be moved aside during the course of the build

Repurposed toys that participants can loan the project

- Dominoes
- Toy cars and ramps
- Marble run tracks
- Marbles and balls
- Cups

How to Make a LEGO WeDo & Scratch Chain Reaction Machine

1. Start by brainstorming a list of "triggers" that will cause the project to go from the physical world to the digital world. One workshop came up with these ideas:

   - Ramp to the distance sensor
   - Ramp -> crash into the the tilt sensor
   - Dominoes
   - A swing
   - Wheels
   - Knock down books
   - Marbles (marble chute)
   - Cards
   - Microphone

2. Next, each participant decides which sensor she or he would like to use in the project. Scratch works with one sensor and one motor attached to the USB hub, so you cannot incorporate both the tilt and distance sensor into your project.

3. Participants should position themselves around the tables on which the chain reaction machines will be built, or an established order of the machines needs to be written down if the machines will be built on cardboard and stored over the course of the build.

4. Start building! Using the LEGO and other materials, start crafting around the physical motion that starts your chain reaction machine. The LEGO WeDo kit does not have a huge amount of LEGO, so improvise. The plan will evolve as it goes along. Use cardboard to build big towers. Combine other materials that might be used to trigger the distance sensor or the tilt sensor. Here is a Matchbox ramp mounted to a cardboard tower.

5. Your next model in your chain reaction machine will contain the distance or tilt sensor that when triggered takes the chain reaction machine into the digital Scratch world. Depending upon your physical model from step 4, it might make more sense to use the tilt sensor than the distance sensor, or vice versa. Connect the LEGO WeDo USB hub to your computer and open Scratch. Use the appropriate tilt or distance sensor blocks and test different models that your physical model from step 4 can interact with. Here, a wall has the tilt sensor connected to the back of it. A toy car could go down the ramp from step 4 and crash into this wall, triggering the tilt sensor and causing Scratch to do something.

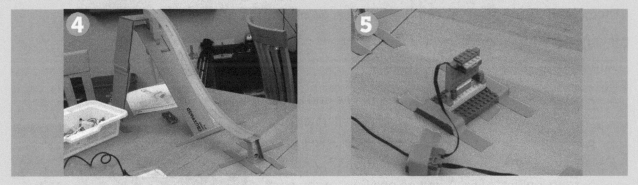

6. Now you need to program your digital world part of the chain reaction machine in Scratch. I urge you not to rush through this part. When you have a large group of people assembled to watch your chain reaction machines in action, it takes very little time for the event to end: marbles and cars roll fast down ramps, and dominoes collapse in a fraction of the time it takes you to set them up. Take advantage of Scratch to stretch the duration of the performance. Surprise your audience with animation, sounds, or narrative.

7. After the Scratch performance of your chain reaction machine, your Scratch program needs to trigger the next model into action back in the physical world. Use the LEGO motor connected to the USB hub to kick over the first in a chain of dominoes, drive a simple vehicle towards a target, or pulley a flag up a pole. Make your chain reaction machine go out with a bang! Here, a motor winds in string that pulls a car towards a distance sensor.

8. Connect the assembled chain reaction machines together and try a test run. You will need to trouble-shoot the physical models and the Scratch programs before the chain reaction machine will go off without a hitch. Collaborate: it takes three people less time to set up a domino run than a single person.

9. Once the participants feel their chain reaction machines are in working order, invite an audience and let the chain reaction machine loose.

Perhaps you can coordinate your participants to use the same Sprite throughout the chain reaction machine? This way a narrative in addition to the physical models might be developed.

Example narrative from a five-day workshop

Chain reaction machines like this are complex combinations of Scratch programming, engineering, crafting, and collaborating to create complex, cacophonous machinery that surprises and delights.

1. A car drives down a ramp, jumping off the end and hitting a wall with a tilt sensor. This causes a car to drive across the screen in Scratch and play a crash cymbal sound. When the car drives off the left edge of the screen, the motor starts and winds in a string, pulling a LEGO car into position for the next machine.

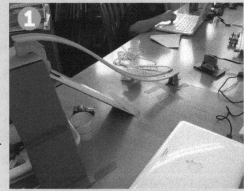

2. Once the distance sensor is activated, in Scratch a plane flies across the screen and crashes to the ground. When the plane crashes, the motor starts and kicks over a domino chain.

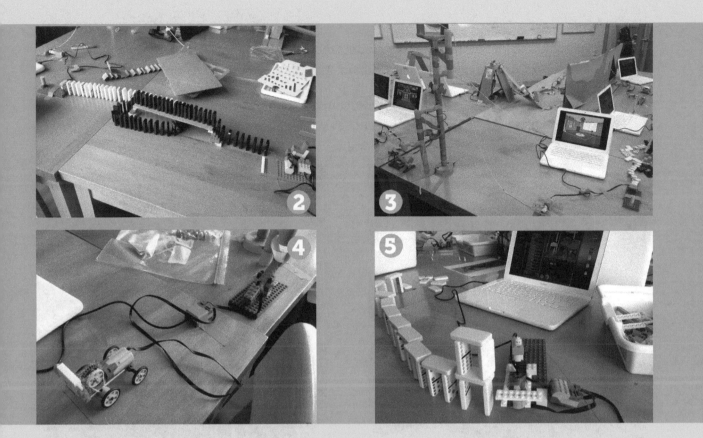

3. The last domino has a tilt sensor taped to it. When the domino falls over, the elephant in Scratch moves towards a slice of chocolate cake until it makes her sneeze, sending the cake flying off the screen and turning on the motor. The motor winds in string attached to a cup on top of a marble chute. The marble falls into a cup mounted to a LEGO arm with a tilt sensor attached.

4. The tilt sensor causes Scratch to animate a dog ambling and barking its way across the screen. When the Scratch dog reaches the left edge of the screen it turns on a motor connected to a physical LEGO dog, which slowly wheels down the table towards the next chain reaction machine.

5. This chain reaction machine's distance sensor reacts to the dog knocking down a set of dominoes. In Scratch, the dog sprite from the previous chain reaction machine reappears, this time "vomiting" on another sprite (this one was programmed by a sixth grade boy). After finishing the dramatic vomit sequence, complete with animation and sound effects, the motor turns on and knocks down another set of dominoes.

6. The falling dominoes trigger the next model's distance sensor. As the car drives across the table, in Scratch an elephant crosses a stream. The car knocks down yet more dominoes.

7. The dominoes trip this model's distance sensor. A lion roars at a construction site. Scratch turns on the motor to lift an arm with a bucket at the end. From inside the bucket, a marble tips onto the track and races down the slope.

8. The marble from the chute is funneled into contact with the next model's distance sensor. In Scratch a ball travels across a soccer field. The motor turns on, knocking a marble down a track, through a cup, onto another track, and into a funnel of LEGO.

9. The distance sensor is activated on the final model. In Scratch, a duck comes down to a gentle landing on the river. The motor simultaneously pulls a LEGO duck with a minifig riding it across the table and raises a flag up a pole.

If you wish to take video of your chain reaction machines in action it is easier to capture each individual machine in action first and edit them into the proper sequence, rather than attempting to chase the machines around the table and capture detail in your video. Of course, you will want a real-time video version, too, but by isolating the machines and running them you can have the maker explain and demonstrate the machine without needing to rush to the next one to catch the machine in action.

LEGO Carnival Games

You can build a variety of carnival games using LEGO WeDo kits, cardboard, and Scratch. Any sideshow game you might play on the midway that uses tilt or distance as part of the game, like knocking over bowling pins or using a mallet to "test your strength," could be adapted to LEGO WeDo and Scratch versions. These projects are simple starters to get you thinking like P.T. Barnum and creating your own "greatest show on earth!"

Challenge Level

All of these projects are easy to build. Young children may need assistance with the hot glue gun or utility knife depending on their abilities.

Materials

- LEGO WeDo Kit and LEGO bricks
- Computer running Scratch 1.4
- Pencil
- Cardboard box
- Cardboard
- Utility Knife
- Ruler

A great time-lapse video of a submarine build is available on the same page where you download the Submarine Rescue Scratch project.

- Hot glue gun
- Hot glue sticks
- Submarine Rescue Scratch Project (http://scratched.gse.harvard.edu/stories/we-do-wedo)

Submarine Rescue Game

1. This first game uses a pre-built Scratch project with a submarine model game controller that you build using LEGO bricks. Your submarine can be simple or complex and look the way you want it to. The model should include the distance sensor. Align the distance sensor so when the submarine is set on the table the distance sensor points towards the table.

2. Additionally, your submarine should have a motor. The motor does not power the model, but you can insert an axle with two of the cams or a gear on it to simulate propeller blades. Both the motor and the distance sensor are plugged into the WeDo USB hub, which you can hide inside the body of your submarine.

3. Download the Submarine Rescue Scratch 1.4 project and open it on your computer. Connect the LEGO WeDo hub in your submarine to the computer with the USB cable.

4. Help the S.S. Papert rescue Scratch the cat! The submarine acts as the game controller. Hold the submarine over the table. As you raise and lower the submarine the S.S. Papert on screen will also raise and lower so you can avoid the fish and other obstacles.

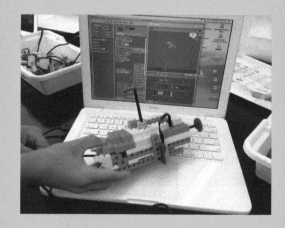

Things to try

1. Remix the Scratch project. Examine the Scratch code and learn how the submarine Sprite works with the distance sensor. Adapt the code to your own project. You can export the submarine Sprite from this project and import it into a new project to have a clean copy. Modify the Sprite's appearance by photographing your submarine model and using the photo as the Sprite's costume.

2. Remix the LEGO model. Build an airplane, a hot air balloon, or a UFO.

"Marble" Tilt Game

The "Marble" Tilt game uses an upcycled cardboard box and strips of cardboard that you form into a maze. Tape the LEGO WeDo tilt sensor to the bottom of the box, make a marble Sprite react to the tilt sensor values, and you have another unconventional game controller.

1. Find a box that is comfortable to hold in your hands. If the box has a top, either remove the lid or use a utility knife to cut the top from the box.

2. Draw maze "walls" in the interior bottom of the box with a pencil. Make sure your maze is solvable!

3. Cut strips of cardboard to the same width. Cut the strips so they match the length of the pencil maze walls you drew. Affix the cardboard strips to the bottom of the box with hot glue, forming three dimensional maze walls.

4. Open Scratch. Click on the Stage in the lower right of the window. In the Stage tabs in the middle of the window, click Backgrounds. Click the Camera button. Hold your cardboard maze in front of the computer's camera and take a photo of the maze.

5. Edit the photo in Scratch. Draw over every wall in the photograph. The line tool set to an appropriate width works well for this step. Make sure each wall is the same color. Trace around the edge of the box, too. You can remove any background in the photograph to make your project look polished.

6. Create your marble Sprite. There are several pre-made ball costumes that you can use, or create your own. Resize the Sprite so it fits in your maze.

7. Tape the LEGO WeDo tilt sensor to the bottom of the box. The cable from the sensor should be oriented so when you hold the box as it appears on the screen the cable is pointed to the bottom of the box. The pegs on the tilt sensor should face up, in contact with the box. Connect the tilt sensor to the USB hub. Tape the USB hub to the bottom of the box.

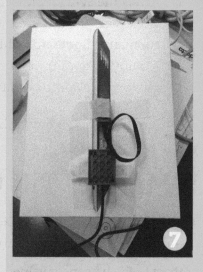

8. Program your marble Sprite to respond to the LEGO WeDo tilt sensor values reported to Scratch. The WeDo tilt sensor reports five values. Hold the tilt sensor so the cable points at you.

   - Not tilted = 0
   - Tilted away from you = 1
   - Tilted to the right = 2
   - Tilted toward you = 3
   - Tilted to the left = 4

9. In the marble Sprite's Scripts tab, add a "When Flag clicked" block and either a "glide 1 secs to x: y:" "go to x: y:" block to place the marble Sprite at the beginning of your maze. Enter the appropriate x and y values for your maze.

10. Add an additional Sprite to act as a goal in the maze. The Sprite can be a simple dot. Make sure the Sprite fits in the maze. Place it at the end of the maze.

11. Write two new procedures to detect whether the marble Sprite is touching the walls and whether the marble Sprite is touching the destination Sprite. The "touching color ?" block is especially useful for these procedures.

12. Connect the LEGO WeDo hub to the computer. Hold the maze game controller in your hands in the proper orien-

tation, with the cable coming from the bottom of the box. Click the Flag to start the project. Can you navigate the marble Sprite to the destination by tilting the maze game controller in the proper directions?

Things to try

1. Incorporate a real marble into the game controller. Experiment with how many steps the Sprite needs to take at each move to best approximate the real speed of the marble.

2. Build more levels. The photograph of the maze box can be rotated four ways. If you want to make the user physically turn the box to mirror how it appears on screen you would need to modify the Scratch code. Physically rotating the box would change the values the tilt sensor reports when you move it in the four directions since the tilt sensor cable no longer points towards you.

Reaching the destination brings the Sprite back to the beginning of the maze in this example. Can you make additional levels? Rotate the existing maze photograph 90 degrees to easily create a second level. Program the marble Sprite to send a Broadcast when it reaches the destination Sprite. The Stage can wait for the Broadcast and switch appearances to the next level when the level one goal is reached.

Carousel Base

Every good carnival has a carousel to ride, and your LEGO WeDO carnival can too. This project walks you through building a solid base for your carousel that you can program to spin at different speeds or directions. Each carousel will look different. You can use additional LEGO and other materials to craft the part of the carousel where people ride, allowing you to be as creative as possible in your carousel design.

1. Connect the LEGO WeDo USB hub to the grey baseplate.

2. Connect the green 2x4 plate to the bottom of the LEGO WeDo motor as shown.

3. Connect the motor to the base plate.

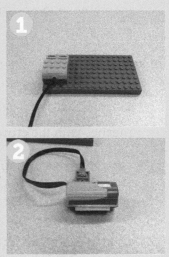

4. Stack two red 1X6 bricks with holes on top of one another. Connect the stacked bricks to the base plate.

5. Insert the small grey axle into the crown gear with the gear teeth facing up. Insert through center hole on 1x6 bricks and into the motor.

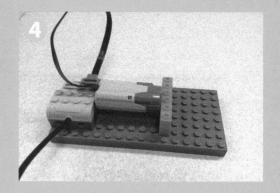

6. Connect a white 2x6 plate to the base plate.

7. Stack two yellow 1x6 bricks on top of one another. Connect the bricks to the base plate.

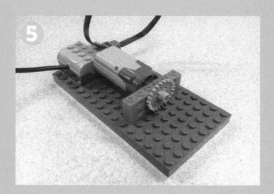

8. Stack one red 1x8 brick with holes on top of the red 1x6 bricks. Stack a second red 1x8 brick with holes on top of the yellow 2x6 bricks.

9. Insert the long axle through the medium sized gear.

10. Insert the axle in the middle hole of the white plate on the base plate. Adjust the position of the gear on the axle so it meshes with the crown gear.

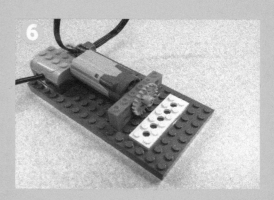

11. Insert the axle through the center of a white 2x10 plate. Attach the plate to the red 1x8 blocks.

12. Insert a green 2x2 rounded brick onto the axle.

13. You can attach the tilt sensor to the USB hub. You can program the carousel in Scratch to change direction and speed based on the tilt sensor values.

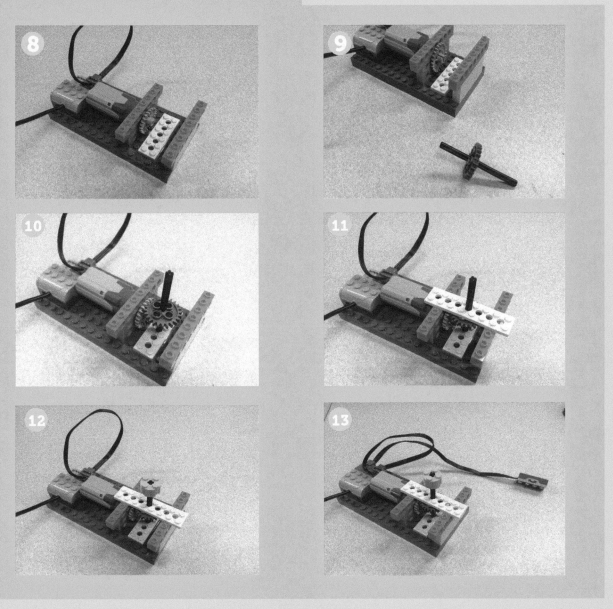

Things to try

1. Build a carousel top. Use more LEGO to build a base, then combine cardboard, pipe cleaners, figurines, and whatever else you have to build a fun carousel top.

2. Experiment with the motor speed to find an optimal carousel speed.

3. Try using the tilt sensor to set both the direction and speed by setting two variables. Think about tilting the sensor left then forward to make the carousel turn counter-clockwise and fast.

Turtle Art Tiles

Turtle Art is a programming language well-suited to exploring geometric art. Why not take the procedures you program on your computer out of the digital world and transform them into 3D printed objects? Through a series of steps you can transform your TurtleArt procedures into 3D printed stamps that you can use to create tiles. Each tile represents a Turtle Art program in tangible form! Whether you stamp Play-Doh or clay that is fired in a kiln, this project is a fantastic way to explore programming, 3D printing, ceramics, symmetry, repetition, Islamic art and architecture, chemistry, and mathematics.

Challenge Level

While this is a multi-step project, it is quite simple and very fun! You can make your Turtle Art program as simple or complex as you are able. Using the 3D printed stamp on Play-Doh or clay gets easier with practice, too. The tiles you create might be temporary, or, depending on your ability and access to equipment, permanent, glazed and fired ceramic works of art.

Materials

- TurtleArt (http://turtleart.org)

- Preview (Mac) or Photos (Windows 8) or a simple image editing application
- Inkscape (http://inkscape.org)
- Tinkercad (http://tinkercad.com)
- 3D printer
- Play-Doh or similar modeling compound
- Toothpick

Optional

- Air hardening modeling clay
- Acrylic paints
- Kiln
- Clay for firing
- Glazes

How to Make Turtle Art Tiles

1. Spend some time programming in TurtleArt to create a pattern that you like. A pattern that repeats can be used to create multiple tiles that could be placed next to one another, like in Islamic tile patterns. Islamic art is famous for intricate patterns that appear complex, but are often simple shapes repeated in symmetrical patterns and rotations. When you have a pattern you like, be sure to save your work.

2. Open a copy of your TurtleArt design in Preview and crop the design. Try to crop your design so tiles could be put together to create a larger pattern. This example uses a square crop, though a rectangular crop would work well if your design is rectangular.

3. Open Inkscape. Although the program looks intimidating, you are using just one feature to convert your .png file to an .svg file, which you can use to create 3D .stl models. Open your cropped TurtleArt design. Choose to embed the image.

4. Single-click the image and go to the Path menu. Select Trace Bitmap.

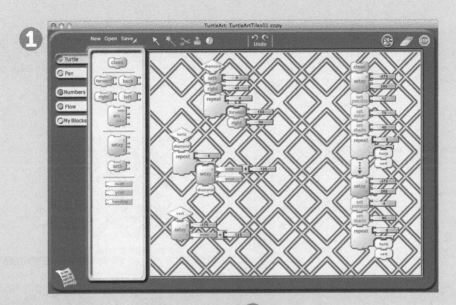

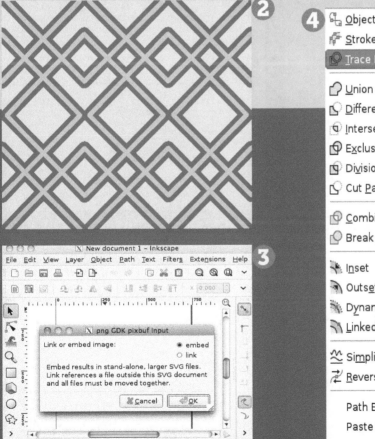

⊕ Object to Path	Shift+Ctrl+C
⊕ Stroke to Path	Ctrl+Alt+C
⊕ Trace Bitmap...	Shift+Alt+B
⊕ Union	Ctrl++
⊕ Difference	Ctrl+-
⊕ Intersection	Ctrl+*
⊕ Exclusion	Ctrl+^
⊕ Division	Ctrl+/
⊕ Cut Path	Ctrl+Alt+/
⊕ Combine	Ctrl+K
⊕ Break Apart	Shift+Ctrl+K
⊕ Inset	Ctrl+(
⊕ Outset	Ctrl+)
⊕ Dynamic Offset	Ctrl+J
⊕ Linked Offset	Ctrl+Alt+J
⊕ Simplify	Ctrl+L
⇄ Reverse	
Path Effect Editor...	Shift+Ctrl+7
Paste Path Effect	Ctrl+7
Remove Path Effect	

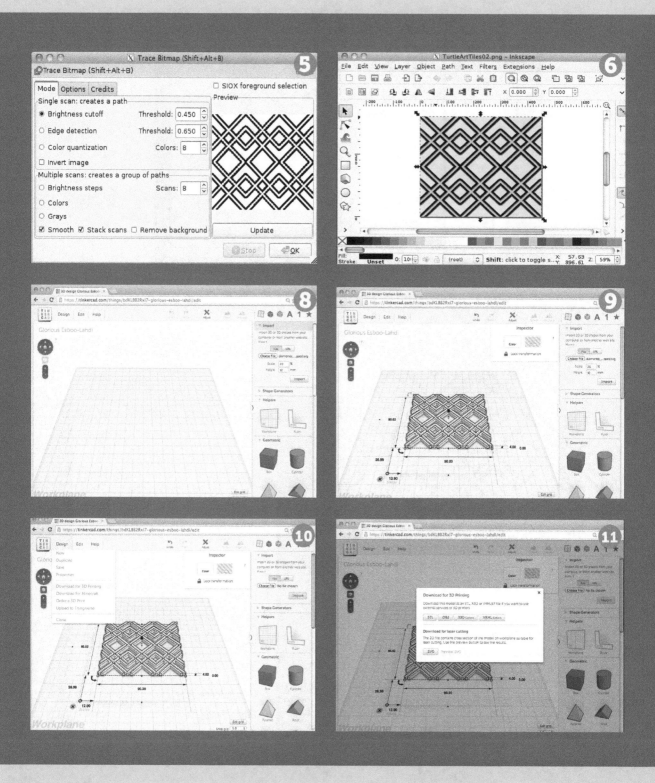

5. Click the Update button to see a preview of the tracing. If nothing appears in the Preview window make sure your TurtleArt procedure was not run in a light color. If it was, go back and try running the procedure in red or blue. Click OK to apply the tracing, then close the window.

6. Your design will now be traced and ready to save in .svg format.

7. From the File menu, select Save As. Make sure you are saving the file in .svg format.

8. Login to Tinkercad.com and create a new design. In the Import field on the upper right side of the window, choose your file and set the scale to 20% and the height to 10mm. Click the Import button.

9. Drag a Ruler from the **Helpers** section in Tinkercad and use it to size your design. Hold down the Shift key on the keyboard and click and drag a corner handle on your design to resize the design with constrained proportions.
    Once you have adjusted the length and width of the tile, you should change the height of the tile to 4 mm.

You will need a stable base for your 3D tile. The tile will be more durable for handling and stamping if there is a solid base under the tile pattern. There are two options for creating the base:

There are a couple of things to keep in mind as you size the tile. First, how big of a tile do you want to create? Second, can your 3D printer print a model that large? I chose to size my tile to about 8 cm X 9 cm, about as large as my Thing-O-Matic printer could print.

*   Create a base the same size as the tile and slip it under the design.

*   Many 3D printers create a raft for you when you print a design. If your printer creates a raft, you do not need to add a separate base.

10. From the Design menu, select **Download for 3D Printing.**

11. Select .STL as the file format. Your model will be downloaded to your computer.

12. Open the downloaded .stl file with the software you use with your 3D printer to slice the model for printing. Here, I opened the file in ReplicatorG.

13. When you generate the GCode for the model, or slice it, make sure you include a raft. The raft holds together the model and makes it easier for you to stamp, and not cookie cut, the modeling compound or clay. If you designed your model with the optional base in Step 9, you can exclude the raft.

14. Print your TurtleArt tile stamp! The more complex the design, the longer the print will take, but it is well worth the wait!

15. Once your have your 3D printed TurtleArt tile stamp you can use it to emboss your design on modeling compound. Play-Doh works well. There is a fine line between pressing too lightly and pressing too hard. Keep a toothpick handy to pick out modeling compound that gets stuck in your model. Experiment with the orientation of the stamp on the clay to create interesting patterns.

> When I ran this project with a fourth grade class I 3D printed a frame slightly larger than the 10 cm X 10 cm tiles that we 3D printed. The students pressed their stamps, removed the stamp, then set the frame around the design and cut around the outside of the frame to get a clean, finished edge.

16. To make more permanent tiles, you can stamp air hardening clay or clay that can be fired in a kiln.

17. Glazing the tile with ceramic glaze helps reveal the beauty of the design.

18. Fire and glaze many tiles to create wall art. Adhere cork to the undersides of fired tiles to make a set of coasters. A collection of different TurtleArt tiles reveals the imagination of the group who created them!

Dungeon Crawl Adventure Game

Imagine a computer adventure game where the hero battles monsters in search of treasure, but the game also responds to the real world! Using Scratch, you can program your dungeon, monsters, and maze to react to light and sound sensors. Scratch can sense the brightness and the amount of noise in the room using the PicoBoard connected to the computer. Program the Stage, Walls, and Sprites to react to different light and sound levels in the room, or to keyboard or mouse input. If the room is too dark, the Stage and Walls are programmed to be difficult to see. Likewise, if the room gets too noisy it excites the monsters to move faster as they track down the hero.

This project will lead you through constructing a light and sound sensor-equipped dungeon with a hero character, one monster, and walls, all of which are affected by the PicoBoard sensors' reading of the light and sounds in the room. The prototype for this example Scratch Project was built over the course of about six hours by a group of twelve middle school programmers. Subsequently, the code was tightened and notes were added in about six additional hours. This is an interesting and extensible project that could occupy a week or a school year.

Materials

- Computer running Scratch 1.4
- PicoBoard (http://sparkfun.com)
- PicoBoard drivers (http://www.picocricket.com/picoboardsetupUSB.html)

Challenge Level

This is an advanced Scratch Project. While you can follow the instructions and build the example blocks to construct a PicoBoard dungeon crawler, you should have a solid understanding of Scratch programming, using variables, and how to use the PicoBoard with Scratch to get the most out of this project. The photographs of the Scratch blocks do not include all the pieces you need to have a completely working dungeon crawler. These directions serve as a start to what hopefully becomes a much larger Scratch Project for you and your friends.

How to Create the Dungeon in Scratch

Create a Scratch 1.4 Project with the following Sprites

- Door
- Wall
- PicoHero
- Hairball
- TheReaper
- ReaperFireball

The Stage

In the PicoBoard Scratch Dungeon Crawler, the Stage reacts to the amount of light in the room. If the room is dark, the stage is dark and details are extremely difficult to see.

Here is an example stage in a relatively bright room. You can see the light sensor value reading at the top of the screen.

1. Draw your Stage. The first level example Stage pictured was one of the example Stages provided with Scratch 1.4 and remixed. Draw additional costumes for your Stage.

2. The second Stage in this dungeon is simply a brown background. Sprites for the PicoHero, Wall, Door, TheReaper, and ReaperFireball all appear on the Stage.

3. Program the Stage to respond to the amount of light in the room. The PicoBoard light sensor reports values between 1 and 100 to Scratch as measurement of the room's brightness. Use these example blocks as a starting point for your Stage. You will have to adjust the values for the amount of ambient light in your room. The brightness effect in Scratch makes the Stage appear dark or light depending on the amount of light the PicoBoard senses. Program the Light Sensor blocks with values between 1 and 100. Set the brightness effect from -50 (for a very dark room) to 20 (for a bright room).

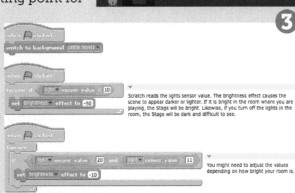

4. Test your Stage blocks. Click the Flag to start the Project. Use your hand to slowly cover the light sensor on the PicoBoard. Confirm that the Stage ranges from bright and visible (uncovered) to dark and difficult to see (completely covered).

The Door

The Door Sprite serves as a goal for the PicoHero to reach on each level. The Door Sprite is responsible for setting a "level" variable that is used by other Sprites.

1. Draw your Door Sprite costume or costumes. You can use a single costume or a different costume for each level of the dungeon.

2. Program the Door Sprite to switch costumes for each level. Additionally, Make a variable for all Sprites, called "level." Use a go to x: y: block to set the Door Sprite's position for the level.

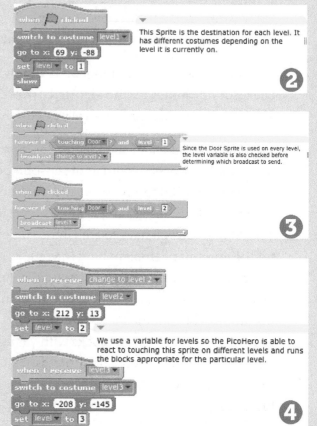

This Sprite is the destination for each level. It has different costumes depending on the level it is currently on.

②

3. Program the Door Sprite to respond to broadcasts from the PicoHero Sprite. The PicoHero Sprite sends a broadcast when it touches the Door Sprite and reaches the end of the level. The Door Sprite responds to the PicoHero's broadcast by changing its costume and relocating on the Stage. Before sending the broadcast, the PicoHero checks the level variable set by the door. Switch to the PicoHero Sprite. Add these blocks to the PicoHero's scripts.

Since the Door Sprite is used on every level, the level variable is also checked before determining which broadcast to send.

③

We use a variable for levels so the PicoHero is able to react to touching this sprite on different levels and runs the blocks appropriate for the particular level.

4. Switch back to the Door Sprite. The Door Sprite has blocks to respond to the PicoHero's broadcasts.

④

5. Test your Door Sprite. Move the PicoHero Sprite to touch the Door Sprite. Make sure the Door Sprite's costume changes. You can place a check next to the "level" variable to display the variable's current status on the Stage.

The Walls

The Walls in this Scratch Project are Sprites. You can build one Wall Sprite then duplicate it, change its appearance, and add functionality with additional procedures. Three examples of Wall Sprites are explained here: stationary, moving, and animated to simulate movement.

1. Draw your Wall Sprite. The Sprite should be relatively small because you should stack many of them next to one another to make complex dungeons. You can use the Grow Sprite button to make large walls out of a single Sprite.

2. Draw additional costumes for your Wall Sprite. Using costumes rather than duplicating a Sprite means all the Walls react in the same way. Here is another costume for the Wall Sprite.

3. Program your Wall Sprite to respond to different light levels. Use the brightness effect block, like you programmed the Stage.

Scratch reads the lights sensor value. The brightness effect causes the Sprite to appear darker or lighter. If it is bright in the room where you are playing, the Sprite will be easy to see. Likewise, if you turn off the lights in the room, the Sprite will be dark and difficult to see.

4. Program the Wall Sprite to respond to the PicoHero's touch. In this example, the Wall Sprite constantly senses whether it is touching the PicoHero Sprite. When the Sprite comes in contact the Wall Sprite sends a broadcast.

You might need to adjust the values depending on how bright your room is.

3

5. Program the Wall Sprite to move. You can add additional complexity to the game play if some of the walls move. Use the motion blocks to make a set of walls move back and forth across the screen.

4

The PicoHero responds to this broadcast.

5

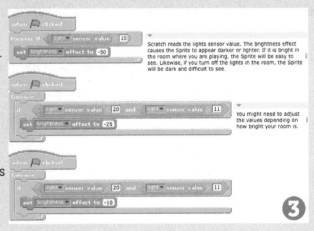

This wall moves!

6. Program the Wall Sprite to animate by cycling between two different costumes. This also makes it appear that the walls are moving. Draw two different costumes for the Wall Sprite.

7. Use switch to costume blocks to alternate between the two costumes.

8. Test your Wall Sprites. Make sure they respond to the light level readings from the PicoBoard. If your Wall Sprites are supposed to move or animate, make sure they do so.

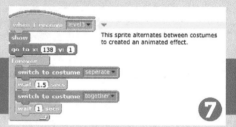

This sprite alternates between costumes to created an animated effect.

PicoHero

The example hero in this Dungeon Crawl has four attributes. It cannot walk through walls, it reacts to the amount of light in the room, it reacts to the amount of sound in the room, and has a self-defense mechanism.

1. Draw your PicoHero Sprite. The Sprite should be relatively small to take advantage of as much dungeon space as the Stage will hold.

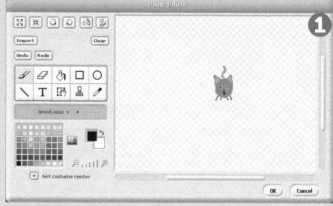

2. Program your PicoHero Sprite to respond to the Wall Sprite's broadcast. When the PicoHero touches the Wall Sprite, the Wall Sprite sends a broadcast. The PicoHero responds to the broadcast by repositioning to where the PicoHero Sprite originally enters the Stage for each level. The PicoHero must check the level variable set by the Door Sprite before relocating itself on the Stage.

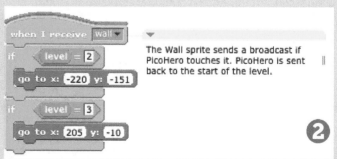

The Wall sprite sends a broadcast if PicoHero touches it. PicoHero is sent back to the start of the level.

3. Program the PicoHero Sprite to react to the amount of light in the room. Since this PicoHero is a cat, it moves quite fast when it is dark in the room, but it moves much more slowly in a bright room. First, make a variable for this sprite only called "speed." Use the PicoBoard light sensor readings to set a value for the speed variable.

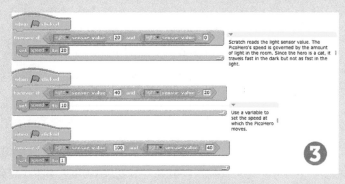

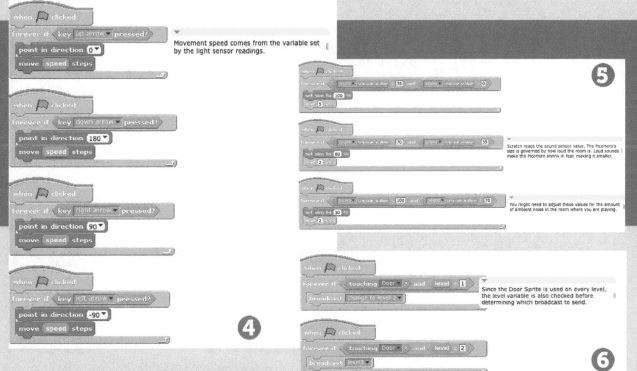

4. Next, program the PicoHero Sprite to move at a speed determined by the light sensor readings and set by the speed variable.

5. Program the PicoHero Sprite to react to sound. This PicoHero responds to loud sounds by shrinking in fear. It uses the set size to % block to change the PicoHero's size for a couple of seconds in reaction to the PicoBoard's sound sensor readings.

6. Make sure your PicoHero Sprite broadcasts when it touches the Door Sprite. You programmed the PicoHero with these blocks when you programmed the Door Sprite.

7. Program the PicoHero's self-defense mechanism. Since this PicoHero Sprite is a cat, it can cough up a hairball. The hairball is aimed using the trackpad or mouse on the computer. Use the when space key pressed block to send a broadcast.

Self defense. Broadcasts to the Hairball sprite.

8. Test the PicoHero Sprite. Make sure you can control its movements with the keyboard. Test the PicoHero's response to the light and sound sensors on the PicoBoard. Make sure you can launch a steered Hairball Sprite.

Hairball

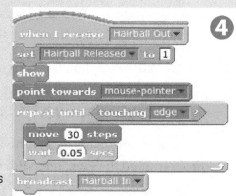

The Hairball Sprite responds to the PicoHero's broadcast and launches towards the location of the cursor on the screen. By aiming the trackpad or mouse before pressing the space key, the player can aim their projectile.

1. Draw the Hairball Sprite. It should be a little smaller than the PicoHero Sprite.

2. Make a variable for all Sprites called "Hairball Released." The initial setup when the Flag is clicked sets the variable state as well as hiding the Sprite and pinning the Hairball Sprite to the PicoHero Sprite until it is released.

Self defense. Broadcasts to the Hairball sprite.

3. Switch to the PicoHero Sprite. Use the when space key pressed block to broadcast "Hairball Out."

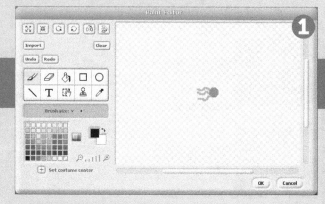

4. Switch back to the Hairball Sprite. Program the Hairball Sprite to respond to the "Hairball Out" broadcast. When the Hairball Sprite receives the broadcast it sets the Hairball Released variable to 1. The Hairball Sprite points

towards where the cursor is currently positioned on the screen. It continues traveling in the direction of the cursor until it reaches the edge of the screen. It then broadcasts "Hairball In."

5. Program the Hairball Sprite to respond to the "Hairball In" broadcast. The Hairball Sprite sets the Hairball Released variable back to 0, hides, then resets its position to that of the PicoHero. This procedure uses the same blocks as the When Flag Clicked procedure.

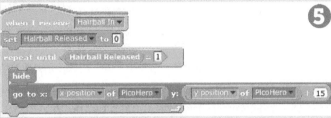

6. Test the Hairball Sprite. Click the Flag to start the Project. Position the cursor somewhere on the stage. Press the space bar: a hairball should shoot from the PicoHero in the direction of the cursor and disappear when it reaches the edge of the screen.

TheReaper

The monster Sprite in this dungeon is called TheReaper. It hurls Fireballs at the PicoHero. It responds to the sound sensor readings from the PicoBoard by relocating itself on the stage when there is a loud sound in the room.

1. Draw TheReaper Sprite. TheReaper Sprite should have two costumes. This Sprite simply raises and lowers its staff in conjunction with releasing a Fireball.

2. Program TheReaper Sprite to always point at the PicoHero Sprite.

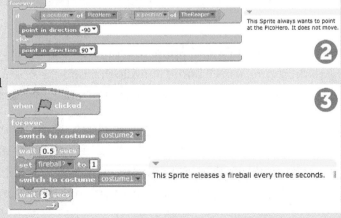

This Sprite always wants to point at the PicoHero. It does not move.

3. Make a variable for this Sprite only called "fireball?" Program TheReaper Sprite to switch between costumes and set the fireball variable to 1.

This Sprite releases a fireball every three seconds.

123

4. Program TheReaper Sprite to respond to the sound sensor values reported by the PicoBoard. When the

TheReaper responds to the sound sensor. If the sound gets louder than "10," TheReaper teleports someplace else on the Stage.

volume gets above a level that you define, TheReaper Sprite will randomly relocate to a different position on the Stage.

5. Test TheReaper Sprite. Move PicoHero Sprite around and make sure TheReaper Sprite remains pointed at PicoHero Sprite. Make sure TheReaper changes where it is on the Stage in a reaction to a sound sensed by the PicoBoard's microphone.

ReaperFireball

The ReaperFireball Sprite responds to the "fireball?" variable and launches at the PicoHero Sprite.

1. Draw the ReaperFireball Sprite. If you choose, you can have many costumes that the Sprite can cycle through when it hits the PicoHero Sprite.

2. Program ReaperFireball Sprite's initial setup. Like the Hairball Sprite, the blocks hide the Sprite and pin it to TheReaper Sprite.

3. Program FireballSprite to respond to the "fireball?" variable. FireballSprite points itself at the PicoHero Sprite then moves towards it. Fireball Sprite might miss PicoHero Sprite and hit an edge because PicoHero can continue to move after Fireball Sprite is released. Finally, Fireball Sprite resets the "fireball?" variable and hides.

4. If you want Fireball Sprite to animate when it hits PicoHero Sprite, program Fireball Sprite to cycle through the costumes. After animating, Fireball Sprite sets the "fireball?" variable to 0.

5. Test the Fireball Sprite. Click the Flag to start the Project. TheReaper Sprite should release a Fireball Sprite about every 3 seconds. The Fireball Sprite should travel in the direction of where the PicoHero Sprite was located when Fireball Sprite was released.

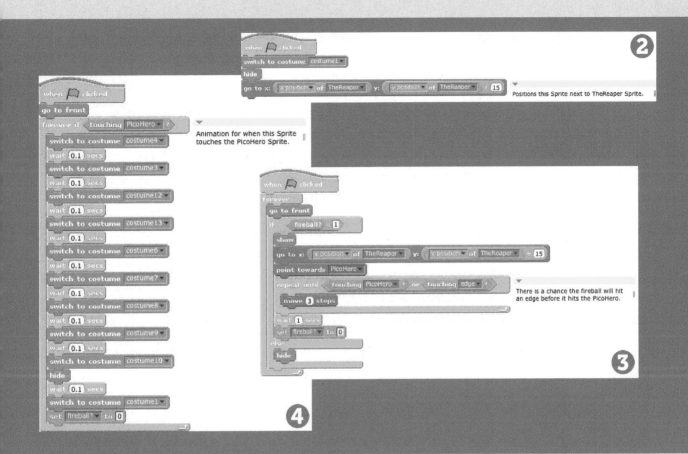

Crawl the Dungeon!

With these Sprites and blocks assembled, you will have most of a working dungeon crawl game. Of course, your dungeon needs more monsters, treasures to claim, and additional levels.

Things to try

1. Develop a hit point system. Using variables, track how many times the PicoHero is struck by the ReaperFireball Sprite. Reduce the PicoHero's hit points every time it is hit by a ReaperFireball. Additionally, make the Hairball Sprite incur damage to TheReaper if it makes contact.

2. Develop additional dungeon monsters. Program the monsters to use the PicoBoard's light and sound sensors. Experiment with different reactions to the sensor readings. If the room

is too loud, for example, make the monster move faster towards the PicoHero than it does in a quiet room. Some monsters might see better in the dark than in the light.

3. Incorporate the PicoBoard button. Use the PicoBoard button to roll "dice" like in Dungeons & Dragons. Encounters with monsters could inflict damage on the monster Sprites or the PicoHero sprites by programming a random number generator that starts and stops when the PicoBoard button is pressed. If the monster Sprites and the PicoHero Sprite are both reading the button press, every Sprite could have a different number generated. The number could be dice rolls for each Sprite to determine damage to hit points.

4. Incorporate Treasure Sprites. When touched by the PicoHero, the Treasure Sprites can set a variable for all Sprites. Monster Sprites can read this variable and rob PicoHero of collected Treasures. Successful completion of the dungeon can be tracked by tallying the number of Treasure Sprites collected during the crawl.

5. Download and remix this Scratch Project. You can find it at http://cmkpress.com/fun/crawl

Crystal Radio Receiver

Talk to people over the age of fifty, particularly someone who was either in the Scouts or interested in electronics, and he or she will have certainly attempted to build, if not successfully, a crystal radio receiver. Using some components you can scavenge around your workshop and a few you might have to order online, you can build a crystal radio receiver. Based in part on the cat's whisker design used by soldiers fighting in the trenches during World War I, these simple radio receivers are fickle but able to pick up sounds from the ether. Build one and see if you can hear radio signals, too.

Challenge Level

This can be considered a hard project. While the assembly of the crystal radio receiver is not difficult, the tools, such as a Dremel and a 3D printer, do require some careful handling and training. This is a perfect project for an adult and a child to work on together, or in a small group that has been trained to use the tools.

Materials

- Toilet paper tube
- About 35 feet of 22 gauge solid insulated hookup wire
- Germanium diode
- Two alligator clips
- Crystal earphone
- Wide rubber band for wire wrapping and radio tuning

- Wire cutters/strippers
- Dremel with grinding attachment
- Scissors

Optional

- Access to a 3D printer
- 3D printed toilet paper tube (model available at http://tinkercad.com/things/0KXg4ibAaxK)
- Acetone or model glue to join the 3D printed toilet paper parts

Steps

1. Choose whether you will use a toilet paper roll or the 3D printed version. The 3D printed version holds up better to wire wrapping but if you are careful the cardboard toilet paper works fine.

2. Carefully poke a hole at one end of the cardboard toilet paper roll. Poke three more holes, in a 3 o'clock, 6 o'clock, and 9 o'clock pattern at the other end of the tube. The 3D printed model has the holes already in place.

Looking at the side of the tube with three holes in it, note the way they are referred to in the directions.
Hole 1 is at 3 o'clock.
Hole 2 is at 6 o'clock.
Hole 3 is at 9 o'clock.

3. Insert an inch of your 35 foot length of 22 gauge wire in the single hole end of the tube. Start winding the wire closely but not overlapping the entire length of the tube.

4. Once the wire is wound around the length of the tube, strip an inch of insulation from the wire and insert it through hole 1 in the tube.

Use a rubber band to hold the wire in place so you can put down the wire and tube as you work.

5. Use a Dremel with a grinding attachment to remove the insulation from a strip of the wire running the length of the tube. Work slowly and do not attempt to remove too much insulation at a time.

6. Cut the 1/8" jack from the crystal earphone. Carefully strip an inch of the insulation from the pair of wires.

7. Put one of the headphone wires through hole 1 on the tube. Wind the headphone wire around the tube coil wire in hole 1, making your wire connections inside the tube.

8. Cut a three foot length of 22 gauge hookup wire and strip an inch of insulation from both ends. Push one end of this wire through hole 1 and connect it to the other two wires. You will have three wires connected inside hole 1: the tube coil wire, the headphone wire, and the three foot hookup wire.

> Unlike an LED, this diode does not have polarity. You can connect to either arm of the diode in the next steps.

9. Carefully bend the arms on the Germanium diode so they fit through holes 2 and 3.

10. Take the second headphone wire, insert it through hole 2, and wind the stripped end around the leg of the Germanium diode.

11. Cut another three foot length of 22 gauge hookup wire and strip one inch of insulation from one end and five inches from the other. Push the five inch stripped length through hole 3 from the inside of the tube to the outside. Connect the last inch of the stripped wire to the Germanium diode in hole 3.

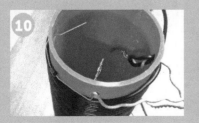

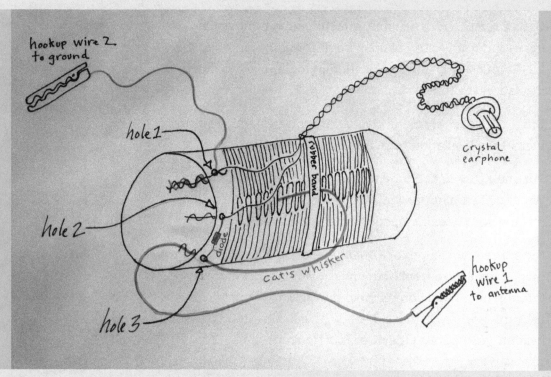

hookup wire 2 to ground

hole 1

hole 2

hole 3

rubber band

diode

cat's whisker

crystal earphone

hookup wire 1 to antenna

12. The rest of the stripped length is the tuning wire. It will touch the exposed wire on the tube coil to tune the crystal radio receiver.

13. Connect alligator clips to the stripped ends of both hookup wires.

Your crystal radio receiver is now built!

Next, you will use a long length of insulated wire as an antenna and the plumbing in your house as your ground to tune your radio and listen for signals.

1. Clip one hookup wire to a long piece of insulated wire that you have removed half an inch of insulation from one end. Use some tape to affix the insulated wire to the wall of the room, up high so it can pick up a signal.

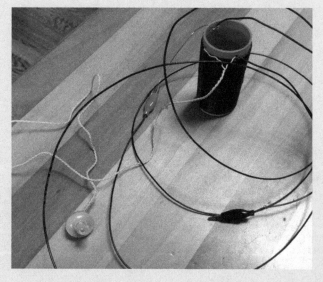

2. Connect the other hookup wire to the cold water shutoff under a sink in your house. If there is not a sink nearby, try connecting the other hookup wire to a heat register. You are trying to ground the radio to the house, so anything nearby that is grounded will work.

3. If you have your earphone in while you are trying to ground your crystal radio receiver, you will hear a faint "click" when it is first grounded.

4. Sit quietly with the earphone in your ear and slowly touch the coil with the "cat's whisker" tuning wire while listening for a signal. You are connecting the short length of wire to the wire coil in different points along the length of the tube.

5. When you find a signal you can use a rubber band to hold the tuning wire in place along the tube coil so you can sit back and listen. To listen to a different station, move the tuning wire to a different place along the tube coil until you find another.

Things to try

1. If you live in or near a large city where there are many radio signals, try holding one of the alligator clips in you hand and attach the other end to the cold water pipe under the sink. You body will serve as an antenna.

2. Crystal radio receivers are affected by the time of day, the weather, and the direction you turn the tube coil. Track your variables to find an optimal listening time, direction, and weather conditions.

3. Use a length of hookup wire to lengthen one hookup from your receiver so you can connect it to the cold water shutoff under the kitchen sink to try to better ground the receiver.

4. Research and build a proper antenna for your crystal radio receiver. There are plans on the Internet. Be careful with your larger antenna. If you are putting this conductive element into the sky, make sure it is properly constructed for the safety of you and your property.

About the Author

Josh Burker was privileged to spend some of his early years near his grandfather, who had a giant carriage shop with countless tools, many of which he taught Josh to safely use at a young age. By second grade he could be found in the garage using a jig saw to cut out Ivanhoe shields and to craft nunchucks from dowels and chain. His interest in woodworking grew and included a January Plan during college spent woodworking. He also organized and co-facilitated a six month long automata workshop that combined woodworking and engineering skills with 3D design and printing.

A LEGO manic since Kindergarten, Josh grew up in a household with many brothers and many LEGO bricks. His LEGO WeDo Scratch Phonograph, first conceived and built at Constructing Modern Knowledge Summer Institute, was published in MAKE: Magazine volume 35. He loves the versatility of LEGO bricks combined with the engineering limitations imposed by the material. Josh has become very interested in 3D design and 3D printing the past couple of years. He marvels at being able to create parts he needs rather than conforming his designs to what connectors or parts are available. He started his foray into 3D printing by completing the build of a MakerBot Thing-O-Matic printer kit and continues to fine tune it to this day.

Josh has been teaching for 15 years and is currently a teacher at an independent day school where he works with students and teachers in grades K-5. Josh also works at a local library maker space, with home schooled students, and at Scratch Day events, leading maker workshops exploring the intersection of technology and crafting. Josh lives in Connecticut with his wife and young son, who loves working on projects with his dada. He holds a Master of Arts in Educational Technology from Pepperdine University and a Bachelors of Arts from Colby College.

You can find him online at http://joshburker.blogspot.com or on twitter @joshburker.

Also from Constructing Modern Knowledge Press

Available from Amazon.com

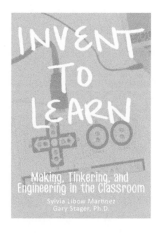

Invent To Learn: Making, Tinkering, and Engineering in the Classroom

by Sylvia Libow Martinez and Gary Stager

Join the maker movement! There's a technological and creative revolution underway. Amazing new tools, materials and skills turn us all into makers. Using technology to make, repair or customize the things we need brings engineering, design and computer science to the masses. Fortunately for educators, this maker movement overlaps with the natural inclinations of children and the power of learning by doing. The active learner is at the center of the learning process, amplifying the best traditions of progressive education. This book helps educators bring the exciting opportunities of the maker movement to every classroom.

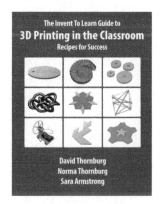

The Invent To Learn Guide to 3D Printing in the Classroom: Recipes for Success

by David Thornburg, Norma Thornburg, and Sara Armstrong

This book is an essential guide for educators interested in bringing the amazing world of 3D printing to their classrooms. Learn about the technology, exciting powerful new design software, and even advice for purchasing your first 3D printer. The real power of the book comes from a variety of teacher-tested step-by-step classroom projects. Eighteen fun and challenging projects explore science, technology, engineering, and mathematics, along with forays into the visual arts and design. The Invent To Learn Guide to 3D Printing in the Classroom is written in an engaging style by authors with decades of educational technology experience.

Sylvia's Super-Awesome Project Book: Super-Simple Arduino (Volume 2)

by Sylvia (Super-Awesome) Todd

In this super fun book, Sylvia teaches you to understand Arduino microcontroller programming by inventing an adjustable strobe and two digital musical instruments you can play! Along the way, you'll learn a lot about electronics, coding, science, and engineering.

Written and illustrated by a kid, for kids of all ages, Sylvia's whimsical graphics and clever explanations make powerful STEM (Science, Technology, Engineering, and Math) concepts accessible and fun.

CPSIA information can be obtained
at www.ICGtesting.com
Printed in the USA
LVHW02s0306190118
563140LV00001B/2/P